THE SENATOR

A remarkable story

Dr Grace Kerry

The Senator
Copyright © 2017 by Grace Kerry.

ISBN: 9781980263906

First Edition: July 2017

DEDICATION

This is dedicated to my ever-cherished parents, Venerable Gabriel and Senator Bernice Kerry for what they gave to the world and me. It is also dedicated to all hardworking mothers throughout the world.

This book is also in memory of my much loved brothers George, Samuel and Patrick.

AKNOWLEDGEMENTS

thank my children for their encouragement throughout the writing of this book, and for their help with proofreading and formatting of the final copy of the manuscript.

I would like to thank all my friends, especially, Agnes Ikazoboh, family and well-wishers for their support at all times. I thank the medical personnel who cared for my mother while she was in the UK for rest and medical care (1996-97) at a B.U.P.A. Private Hospital in Cardiff. They were the Orthopaedic Consultant, Mr. David Pemberton; the Ophthalmologist, Mr. Nicholas Hawkeworth; our optician, Mr. Christopher Ellis; Staff Nurse, Barbara Evans and our GP Dr. Mark Wiltshire.

You will always be remembered!

CONTENTS

PREFACE

* * *

I believe that writing this book will shed some light on the nature of women's role in Nigerian politics and the family as depicted in this biography of my mother' life.

I was compelled to write this book because not many know or talk about women in politics in the fifties and sixties in Nigeria. For example, a Nigerian publishing house that I approached about publication of this book, asked, "Who is Mrs. Kerry"? "That's the point", I said. Mrs. Kerry was a giant figure, socially, ecumenically and politically in Nigeria, and her legacy is worth publishing.

Mrs. Kerry was a rare breed, born to lead, to love and to achieve. There is really no glamour in politics, but she brought glamour, elegance and fairness to everything she did, be it her activity in the Senate, verdicts in the Customary Court, fighting for widows, the poor, the lonely, the forsaken and the powerless. She triumphed in all these, in the shadow of back-to-back military coups, civilian government and minimum resources.

My mother's life is linked to the present. People are kinder to me when they learn I am my mother's child. She loved and nurtured people; saw to their needs and was always true. She never failed in her duty as a daughter, sister, wife, mother, grandmother and aunt. Many who knew her regularly showered her with gifts.

I learned a lot about the past from my parents. My mother constantly told us the story of her life and family, not that she wanted me to write a book about her life; though she was delighted when I told her I was going to do so. The anecdotes about her childhood, her parents, her growing up and marriage always crept into our conversations. She helped us get on with our lives. She was persistent and constant in our lives, for moral and financial succour. My mother helped people to succeed and was the wind that blew us higher to reach for the skies. Her passing changed our lives forever.

I have tried to be as objective as I can in writing this book and to write an honest account of what I know about my mother. This biography is based on what was relayed to me, by my mother, grandmother, father, what I witnessed about my mother's life and what I gathered from the Kerry family archive. Some names have been altered for obvious reasons.

It took me a longer time to write this book than I anticipated, due to the poignancy and joy of raking through my mother's life for details for the book. I cannot adequately express my joy at its completion.

"There is no fear in love... perfect love casts out fear"
I John, 4:18.

INTRODUCTION

* * *

This is the synopsis of the biography of Mrs Bernice U. Kerry (1912 – 2005), who was one of the first lady senators in the First Republic of Nigeria, 1963-1966.

Mrs. Kerry was a miracle child, who rose from humble beginning to marry a teacher, Gabriel Kerry, who himself rose to become Archdeacon of the Anglican Church. She became deeply involved in the work of the church and subsequently politics throughout her life' especially, in the welfare of young girls, women and children. She was renowned as an industrious, self--reliant and successful businesswoman in the timber and scrap metal industry. It was entirely by popular vote that Mrs. Kerry was appointed the First Republic Senator of Mid-West State (later Bendel State) in Nigeria's Federal House of Parliament

Following the 1966 coup and the subsequent Nigeria/Biafra conflict, Mrs. Kerry was tried by the Military Tribunal at the end of the war for feeding hungry Biafra soldiers. She was a champion of the oppressed and a philanthropist. In her role as Customary Court Judge, she gave an historical minority judgement in a land case, which was incorporated into the Nigerian Law.

In 1976, Mrs. Kerry represented the Benin Diocese of Nigeria at the Mother's Union Centenary celebration in the UK, where she met Her Majesty Queen Elizabeth 11. She received many awards in her lifetime and was a Justice of Peace and Christian Knight of the Order of St Mary.

For many reasons, this story needs telling. I believe in addition to being a fascinating read, this book can be a viable and valuable text for students in schools and other educational institutions for the following reasons. Mrs. Kerry's history sheds light on a period spanning almost a hundred years. In this regard, my book documents the role(s) and status (and subsequent influence) of women in Nigerian society during that time. For historians and social-political commentators, it will be the first of its kind to give insight into the *Realpolitik* of twentieth century African diplomacy during a decade of great political and cultural change and upheaval.

As I wrote in the preface, I have been as objective as I can in writing this book and I can honestly say that by anyone's standards, Mrs. Kerry was an outstanding political figure with a remarkable story similar in narrative to the arc of a fairy tale. She overcame the odds to transgress the borders of gender politics. She was the girl who, through and in extraordinary circumstances became the woman who gave much to her people and her country.

This biography is a vivid and engaging historical document of the period in question and focused industry can contribute to the betterment of individual lives and the greater good of a nation as a whole. I have written this as a tribute to a positive role model, an exemplar, a wise formidable politician, and an outstanding daughter, mother and friend.

1: IN THE BEGINNING

✱ ✱ ✱

"Before I formed you in the womb I knew you,
before you were born I set you apart."
Jeremiah 1:5

The arrival of white missionaries in Southern Nigeria in the late eighteenth and beginning of the nineteenth century caused some upheaval, both positively and negatively in the social and cultural life of the people. The negative aspect has been clearly depicted in Chinua Achebe's 1958 novel "Things Fall Apart", a narrative which tells of the coming of the white man to Eastern Nigeria and the debilitating effect on the life of the people, with the slave trade, and the division and fracture of the indigenous society due to the arrival of the Christian religion. On the positive side, however, missionaries introduced formal education through Christianity and those, such as Mary Slessor abolished the practice of human sacrifices and the killing of twin babies, which were endemic in some parts of South Eastern Nigeria.[1]

---

[1] Mary Slessor was a Scottish missionary who was sent to the Calabar region in Nigeria in 1876, an area of West Africa that no European had ever been to before.

My maternal grandparents were amongst those who benefitted from the arrival of the missionaries to their native Igbodo in 1903. The birth of my mother (a few years later) followed that momentous event after her parents' conversion to Christianity. Igbodo is a small rural town on the west bank of the River Niger, located in a remote part of what was then Western Nigeria, 15 miles west of Asaba, with Onitsha, three miles away on the east side across the River Niger. The arrival of the gospel to Igbodo was the product of the 1857 Niger Mission. Miss Fanny Dennis, a twenty-three year old spinster from England and Miss Ross who was of similar age and from Scotland were two of the carriers of the gospel news to Igbodo. Miss Fanny was tall with an attractive face and Miss Ross was petite and equally attractive. My mother arrived in the world some years after the missionaries came to Igbodo. This child of hope and destiny was born to converted Christian parents, Rachel Akpato Okonye and Isaiah Badi Okonye. The life of my mother is a narrative, which deserves to be told, to my children and to the rest of the world, because it is a most remarkable and inspirational story.

Igbodo is within the range of the African tropical rainforest and has a hot climate even during the rainy season, which is usually from April to August, and into early September. The sun and rain in their seasons beat down with equal vengeance. All those years ago, the town was cloaked in dense lush forests with only dust roads and bush tracks running through them. Wildlife dawn choruses of cockerels, wild guinea fowls, the cuckoo and other wild birds told the time, heralding the dawn of day, informing the rural dwellers it was time to go to the farm or to the village market. The position of the sun also indicated the time of day by the length of its shadows, which was, and still is, shortest at midday and longest in the evenings. Daybreak is usually beautiful in Nigeria with birds singing amidst luscious vegetation and beautiful sunrise. The air is filled with the fragrance of this natural environment.

These people spoke a dialect of the Igbo or Ibo language and were sometimes referred to as Western Igbos or Ibos. The inhabitants were also known as Aniocha people due to the colour of their soil which was red.

Akpato, my grandmother (her precise date of birth is unknown) was the eldest of eleven children, and her youngest sibling, Anene, a little girl, was only two years old when their mother died. Their father had died a year before. So my grandmother became a sole carer, left to bring up her ten younger surviving siblings, all of whom she outlived, though one of them, Nathaniel, lived long enough for me to have known him. When we visited my granny at Igbodo as children, my mother's uncle Nathaniel used to bring baskets of seed yams for my mother whenever he returned from the farm. My grandmother was, possibly, in her early twenties, tall, pretty, strong and confident and hard-working, when she took on that very significant responsibility. Her great heartache came in 1918 when her baby sister, Anene, who she had raised when they were left orphans, died suddenly of the influenza that swept the world, during the First World War. Anene was engaged to be married to Mr Dibia, the first educated Forest Guard (similar to a Park Ranger) from Igbodo. She was only eighteen years old. My mother remembered Anene well.

Married life was very difficult for my grandmother, to say the least because she didn't have a child of her own it is believed, until well into her early forties, when my mother arrived. By now my grandmother's contemporaries were becoming grandmothers! Everyone, including herself, had given up hope of her ever experiencing the joys and pains of motherhood. Her husband, a strong, slightly built good-looking farmer, wanted children to help on the farm and showed little sympathy. This was because according to our native law and custom, females, from the age of eighteen onwards were (and still are) expected to marry, settle down and bear children; motherhood providing women with influence, authority and respect. Consequently, childless women were looked down upon and treated with disdain. My grandmother desperately wanted a child!

Akpato, whose name meant "three bags", because her father had said that anyone wanting to marry his daughter would pay three bags of money, often told me the story of her conversion to Christianity. It happened quickly after years of childlessness. One hot day in 1910, her cousin Adafor informed her she saw a huge crowd of people in the market square. The news was that there were strange people who looked like albinos, (although they were not), speaking to, or rather shouting at the crowd in the market place. Out of curiosity the two cousins hurriedly got dressed and rushed to see and hear what was going on.

As they approached, the preaching stopped, replaced by a rapturous rendition of the hymn "Nnukwu dibia nonso kita" ("The great Redeemer is nigh") Akpato could see two white men and one white woman, with two black men who turned out to be interpreters, holding fat books which she and Adafor were later informed were called *Bibles* and contained the words of God. The crowd and preachers were all swaying in time to the hymn. When the music ended, one of the white men commenced again to preach the word of God. It was a very hot day and there in the blistering heat, the crowd listened. These preachers told how God sent his son Jesus into the world to die on the cross in order to save the world, and how if they believed in Jesus, He (Jesus) would heal their ills, forgive their sins and bless them with whatever they prayed for.

"Believe!" they roared in turn with religious fervour, "come to Jesus, be baptised, destroy all your idols and be saved!"

My granny said she had never seen anything like it before. She was totally mesmerised. She loved telling her grandchildren this story and I could picture it better as I grew older, because it was similar to the emotions I felt when I attended the American evangelist Rev. Billy Graham's convention at Ibadan, Nigeria in 1960. I was a student at the United Missionary College (UMC) for teachers in Ibadan, and our white teachers gave us one British shilling each to take a taxi to the stadium where the convention was taking place. The experience was transformational! I was totally overcome, especially as Billy Graham was not only a charismatic preacher, he had the classic look of a Hollywood film star!

The white Christian missionaries believed that Christianity was the supreme force for and the primary source of the improvement and civilisation of the human race, with, as W.H Taylor writes, "a special duty to regenerate a benighted Africa." [2] The missionaries preached and demanded monogamy where polygamy was endemic and central to the wealth of the Igbo society.[3] Additionally, they wanted all inanimate and animate objects that were worshipped to be destroyed and they even disapproved of some traditional dances and dress codes. I remember my father relating how those who had converted to Christianity accompanied the missionaries through the villages to burn idols. Idols were thrown into "missionary bonfires" lit in the village square or marketplaces. However, while many who

---

[2] Taylor, W.H, (1984) "Missionary Education in Africa reconsidered: The Presbyterian influence and educational impact in Eastern Nigeria 1846-1974, *African Affairs*, Vol. 83, no.331, (April, 1984) pp.189-205).
[3] Traditionally, prior to the dominance and influence of large-scale western industrialisation polygamy, routinely organised and sanctioned by local tribes in Igbo land, was promoted as a means to ensure productivity in a predominantly agricultural society. The more wives one had, the more potential there was for more children, children that would one day grow up to become workers. In those days, productive cooperation within towns and villages was practiced such that the material benefits acquired by a particular family became profitable to the society as a whole.

had listened to the missionaries were converted, some stuck to their traditions and faith. So it came about that in Nigeria in particular, and West Africa in general, a wide variety of religious beliefs emerged, including Christianity alongside Islam, whilst some traditional African religions remained.

"The preachers were all very white", my grandmother said, "with straight hair and "long noses". The villagers were puzzled, confused and enraptured in equal measure. The missionaries were also so impeccably dressed with starched and gleaming sleeveless khaki shirts and khaki shorts. The men also wore huge hard brown safari hats locally called "ogomabala", to ward off the relentless heat of the sun. "Ogomabala", the meaning of which is, "my in-law is rich", later became a badge of wealth and enlightenment in my area. If your father happened to possess an "ogomabala", this symbolised his gentrification. My grandmother said that at first people thought the preachers had no toes, because they were wearing shoes. The tale around the village was that these strangers were " nmadu, ma fa enwero mkpisi-ukwu", which means, "they were humans but they had no toes".

The most amazing thing about these white people, according to my grandmother was that "they even had nice small clean pieces of cloth with which they used to blow their noses and mop their sweaty foreheads".

My granny, though tall, had the fuller figure many Nigerian men appreciate. Her husband on the contrary was not tall but strong. My grandmother approached the missionaries cautiously and stopped beside one of them (later identified as Miss Ross) and waited until the end of the session to ask her a burning question. By now people were clapping and singing in the heat. Through an interpreter, my grandmother said, rather timidly, "I'm longing for a baby. "I want Jesus to bless me. Please pray for me to have a baby."

"God will answer your prayers and give you a baby," Miss Ross reassured her.

"If and when God gives me this baby as you promised, will you take the baby from me?" my granny asked with curiosity.

Smiling sympathetically at my grandmother, the missionary replied emphatically, "Oh no! Your baby will always belong to you."

"Alright, I'll come with you. I'll go to church. I'll worship this almighty God till the end of my days."

Thus my grandmother's journey with God and the church began. She, her husband Badi and her surviving sibling, were admitted, with the other converts, into the Church Missionary Society (CMS) church. She was baptised and christened Rachael, pronounced "Hechelu" by the locals. Her husband was christened Isaiah, pronounced locally as "Azaya".

The open-air session lasted about two hours and as the crowd began to disperse in the evening at the end of it all, the heavens opened and they were all drenched, as if, my grandmother said, to "wash away our sins"[4].

The first real church building was set up in Igbodo in 1910, two years before my mother was born. Before then, church gatherings were held in the homes of two converts (Paul Onai or Mary Alolo) or in the open air. The Christians also held an ecclesiastical Christian walk once a month on Eke market day to preach the gospel. There were market days which came around every four days in the local area, namely, Nkwo, Eke, Orie and Afor. Even today in the villages, a boy born on any of these market days is called either, Okonkwo, Nweke, Okorie or Okafor. If it is a girl, she is named Adankwo, Adaeke, Adaorie and Adafor.

In that remarkable year 1912, on a bright, sunny beautiful day in June (though it was the height of the rainy season), a much

---

4 Acts 22:16, (King James Version).

longed-for baby was born to my maternal grandparents. This baby girl was named Uwanugo-ozioma, meaning, "the world has heard this good news". Her mother's pet name for her was "Nwaga", which means, "the child of a barren woman" because she perceivedd herself as barren until her baby arrived. My grandmother said she did not know or believe she was pregnant and did not understand the bump in her tummy until the baby began to flutter and kick. It was my mother alright!

"My baby was born, bright-eyed, very alert, with a smile etched on her face. She had a kind of strong positive aura around her", my grandmother told me. "She was a lovely creation, long-limbed even at birth and my heart ached with so much love for my baby." Rachael was about forty-two years old when she gave birth. Mother and baby grew closer by the day and Rachael was unaware that her baby was destined to achieve so much in the world. When my mother went to school, her mother would wait for her at the end of the day on the dust road in front of their thatched home. She guessed her state of health from afar. If her child was skipping home she knew she was well and happy but if she was strolling languidly home her mum knew something was amiss usually to do with the state of her health - probably she had fallen ill at school with malaria.

The missionaries were at hand to help my grandmother and her family. Her baby was named and christened Bernice Uwanugo! As my grandmother testified, the day when her daughter came into the world was beautiful and glorious as if to set the scene for the rest of my mother's life.

The activities of the Church Missionary Society spread through Nigeria and Africa at large in the late eighteenth and early nineteenth century. From the Church Missionary Society (CMS) in London emerged the Church Missionary Society for Africa and the East, whose mission it was, "for every Christian to endeavour to propagate the knowledge of the gospel to the 'heathen"[5].

The establishment of a school in Igbodo followed the setting up of the church in 1910. The school was one of the first primary schools in that region at the time. The persecution of the missionaries and converts gathered pace in 1912 when my mother was three months old, so my grandmother and her baby, with other converts fled through the bush to Idumuje-Ugboko, a village six miles east of Igbodo where the missionaries were based. They returned a year later to Ogige Ndi-Uka (the Christian compound) in Ndobu village of Igbodo, where they settled on a big piece of land, exclusively reserved to accommodate about three hundred families of Christian converts. These converts drew strength from one another and their faith. These were dark and hard times but the Christians were happy. They had found faith and succour and my mother was destined to grow up in that environment. All new converts were usually given Old Testament Biblical names at their baptism, names such as Nicodimus, Amos, Obediah, Enock, Zepora, Hilda, Jedidiah, Jeremiah, Zephenaiah, Isaiah, Ezekiel, Dorcas, Nehemiah and Abraham.

Four years after my mother was born, my grandmother, now almost middle-aged, conceived again and had twin boys. The second twin died at birth but Obadiah, known as Obed, survived. Before my uncles were born, having twins was a taboo in some rural areas of Nigeria and my surviving uncle was allowed to live because in 1913, a pair of twins were rescued by Christians from the bush where they were dumped. They were nurtured and they survived. It was then realised that twins were a blessing and not a force for evil. Obed, my uncle, later became a successful court clerk, a prestigious position in those days. A gentle giant, my uncle Obed was tall, good-looking and built like a powerhouse and he was the best wrestler in the whole

[5] Eugene Stock, Yes Magazine, (excerpts from) "The History of the Church Missionary Society, 1899", accessed 8th October 2010.

area, a great farmer and an accomplished hunter. He had fifteen children from four marriages and loved them all the same. My uncle taught all his sons to hunt and farm, though they were all educated. My mother and her brother were very close, looking out for each other and working together all their lives. They consulted with each other on many issues and my mother brought up and educated almost all of his children. My mother and uncle were the greatest of friends until my uncle passed away in 1982. It is believed that excessive drinking shortened his life!

My mother started school aged about eight, which was common in her time. A precious child, her mother clung to her. She was a prodigious little girl, articulate and feisty. Even at a very young age, the compassionate aspect of her nature was evident. She was sporty and also had a glorious singing voice. With her long limbs and slim figure, she was enchanting to behold. She had silky dark skin, dark smiling eyes, long eyelashes, rosebud lips, a long neck and a graceful nose set in a beautiful round face.

She blossomed more and more as she grew older. Miss Ross was never far away. The missionaries loved her, because her mind was sharp. She learned fast. From her earliest years, her presence lit up the room and she was always like a ray of light and sunshine. Her tight curls grew fast and plentiful and her mother used to part her hair in the centre of her head and plait it down in a straight pig-tail style to reach the base of her neck.

My mother's father, Isaiah Badi, left home shortly after Obed was born. He went in search of work (usually labouring jobs) in a place called Sapele, in the Delta area of Nigeria. This was about sixty miles from home and a week's trek to that part of the State where he knew no one. However, it was unthinkable to simply stay at home watching his family starve. The only way to keep alive in those days was to live off the land and it was sometimes a catastrophic experience when (as was sometimes the case) the harvests failed due to drought, locust infestation which came in large clouds and destroyed crops and vegetation or any other unexpected natural disasters. Life was tough for my mother, her mother and her little brother. Some days they had nothing to eat except roast dry corn or "akala-oka" (dry corn, pounded into a thick paste, with salt and a little water, and fried in little balls in palm oil). "Akala-oka" is still eaten in my region today but in a more refined form with eggs, prawns and onions beaten into the mixture and fried in olive or vegetable oil. Hunger and famine were endemic in those days. Few were exempt. People's way of existence was simple and their wants were few and easily supplied by nature. Agriculture was the major employment and everyone, male, female and children were involved in it. Locally made hoes, shovels and machetes were the main work instruments. They grew cotton and spun the fibre to make the original local cloth which people tied round their waist or chest and knotted in front. Local mats for sleeping and sitting were made from palm fronds and reeds, gourds were grown and harvested, cleaned out and used to store food and water. Earthen ware pots were used for cooking and storing water and wood was used for cooking. Mud floors were kept clean and fresh by washing them with bits of soft banana leaves soaked in muddy water. There were many self taught improvisations to make life easier for people. They had beds too, built of mud, and raised to about three to four feet above the floor. People placed locally-made mats on these mud beds to sleep on. Such raised platforms could be seen in other rooms for sitting and relaxing. Small low wooden stools were made for women to sit on during cooking. My grandmother taught me how to make all those things (except the wooden stools) and I loved learning from her

My mother and her brother never saw their father again until she was eleven and her brother seven. When my maternal grandfather returned to the village and people ran with excitement to welcome him, his children did not recognise him and he did not recognise them. My mother and her brother ran past their father in all the excitement. They had grown so tall too. It can only be imagined what my grandmother went through in the absence of her husband in those harsh days, bringing up two young children on her own. My mother often told me of how men would pick fights with my grandmother because her husband was away. My grandmother fought back like a tigress and lost a few teeth through these unfortunate encounters. Her marriage was still unhappy after her husband returned. She was more hardworking than her husband and more ambitious for her children, qualities that my mother inherited. My grandparents constantly fought physically, and for that reason, my mother vowed that she would never allow any opportunity for a fight with her husband, let alone in front of her children.

In my mother's time, only Christians sent their children to school and only when they could afford it or if they believed schooling would benefit them and their children. Generally, only girls were less likely to be sent to school. They stayed home to support their mothers in the home, farm or market, until they got married. So, most children, usually Christian children, started schooling whenever possible, and that could be between six to fifteen years old. Even at fifteen, children were unworldly and young for their age. My own father ran away to school when he was about ten years old. He hated working on the farm. He was born for academia, though his parents didn't realise it then.

My mother attended the CMS Central Primary School in Igbodo until she was fifteen and in Standard Five. She then moved to St Monica's Girls' School (or Ugwu-Ogba as it was also known) in Ogbunike, near Onitsha in Eastern Nigeria.[6] The reason for this move will be explained later.

---

[6] Colonial primary schools in Nigeria at that time went from standard 1

By the time my mother left Igbodo Central School, she was well known by teachers, schoolmates and people in her hometown and surrounding villages because she was involved in many church activities, as well as her schoolwork. She sang beautifully and was in the church choir. She was daring and active. My father, Gabriel Ikeduba Kerry, was already a "pupil teacher" as they were known in those days, and had heard about my mother. Pupil teachers were clever primary school leavers who were recruited into teaching. David Diai, a teacher, who later became a clergyman, was my father's mentor. Mr Diai, with the white missionaries, brought the gospel to Owerre-Olubor, my father's little town. He told my father about a beautiful promising young girl whom he felt would make a perfect missionary wife for him.

First, my mum had to attend St Monica's Girls' School as a prospective clergyman's wife in preparation for missionary life. That was how my mother came to attend the prestigious St Monica's Girls' School. My mum, as usual, excelled in her studies, sports, needlework and singing. In fact she excelled in many things, because, as Miss Ross told my father, "Bernice always gives one hundred percent to everything she does."

The missionaries kept in close contact with my mum. In fact, St Monica's was akin to a finishing school and it was also recommended at that time, that any young girl betrothed to future leaders such as headmasters, politicians and clergymen would be sent to St Monica's Girls' School to be educated, mainly by white missionaries. It was customary for the future husbands to pay the girls' school fees and my father did exactly that for my mother and he said she was worth it! There was also medical work at Iyi-enu hospital nearby, a small hospital

---

to 6 and children went to school, when it was convenient for their parents. For example, when I went to school, I had teenagers in my primary classes and schools were happy to accommodate any such pupils.

opened by missionaries in 1908, where my mother helped out after St Monica's, while getting ready for married life. Dr Barthey, a tall warm and kind man was one of the doctors talked about a lot by my mother, as well as Miss Ross. To get to this school and hospital, my mother would trek, accompanied by her brother or uncle Nathaniel, or occasionally taken on a bicycle from Igbodo or travelled in an open-backed rickety lorry on a dust road (full of potholes) of sixteen miles to Asaba, cross the Niger River by boat, which was often hazardous, and then trekked further or be taken on a bicycle by a relative to her school.

The Diocese of the Niger was created in 1922 within the jurisdiction of the Niger Delta, of which Bishop Larsbery was the bishop in charge. The CMS Teachers' Training College in Akwa, where my father was later to undertake his teacher training was founded at the same time. Miss Ross (her first name remains unknown as was common in those days) was my mother's guardian until her marriage. My mother was to complete her primary education (which was standard Six at that time, after leaving Igbodo in standard Five) at St Monica's Girls school in 1930. That level of primary education at that time, was as sound (and some might argue, even better) than current secondary education in Nigeria. At St Monica's, my mother met Flora Azikiwe, the future wife of Dr Nnamdi Azikiwe. Dr Azikiwe was the first post-colonial political President of Nigeria, and was also known as "Zik" of Africa. He brought real politics to Nigeria and the Cameroon. My mother and Mrs Azikiwe became life-long friends.

So began my mother's journey towards her calling. My father told me that he fell in love with my mother at first sight. My mother fell in love with him immediately too, though they never really expressed things in such romantic terms in those days. A fine figure of a man, my father was a well-built 5ft 10ins tall. He was light in complexion and had a small gap between his well-formed two front upper teeth. Though softly spoken and sometimes a little shy, he was an exceptionally powerful and charismatic preacher. He was determined too, especially when he believed in what he was doing. As soon as he could read and write, he had his initials, "GIK", tattooed on his inside forearm above his left wrist. This intrigued us a lot as children. My mother had many suitors, which she rejected but she knew she had met the right man as soon as she set eyes on my father.

My father was from the neighbouring village of Owerre-Olubor, eight miles to the East of Igbodo. As a "pupil teacher", he was fairly well known to my mother's family but my grandmother actually wanted her daughter to marry someone from her town Igbodo. To my grandmother, Owerre-Olubor was too far! She wanted her daughter near her at all times. She did not even want her daughter to go to St Monica's in the first place but she realised there was something special about her daughter and knew that in her education there was an opportunity that would benefit the entire family, especially when it resulted in an educated man being interested in marrying her daughter and willing to pay her school fees as well. Besides, the missionaries still had a lot of influence on the early Christians. My maternal grandparents' faith in Christianity grew with intensity by the day, and they believed implicitly in the power and will of God. To them, their religion and faith in God held their lives together.

My mother matured into a tall (5ft 10ins), slim, stunningly beautiful woman. She was always immaculately dressed, pleasant, happy and cheerful. Most of all, she loved life! She had such a passion for life and was very compassionate. My mother was exquisitely beautiful, indeed the most attractive person I've ever known. Moreover, her beauty was more than skin-deep. People felt at ease with her, because she always had a positive attitude. She was thought to have an innate wisdom and as such was always sought after as trusted counsel. Her arms were always outstretched to hug when she met people. "Good to see you", she would beam, "how are you my child? How are your children? Is all well with your family? Have you all eaten today? Has your child been to school today?" and so forth. She loved people and people warmed to her. Her charm and friendliness were infectious and she was such good company that people were attentive to her. She relished challenges and her life was full of adventure, which she often sought. My mother's capacity for friendship was legendary. She was gifted with rich laughter, child-like warmth and a quick and effortless sense of humour. All these qualities combined to make her a unique human being.

My mother taught me the best values in life: hard work, honesty, staunch loyalty and how to love others and ones-self. She loved to see me and I loved her company more than I can say. She was the mother *par excellence* and a fantastic role model for everything a wife should be.

The relationship between my mother and us, her children, was close and loving. She was everything to us and we cherished her love. My children adored her too. She told us the truth, whether we listened or not and I trusted her judgement. I've met people who wished my mother was their mother. She was constantly giving, always prepared to share whatever she had (food, time, advice and money) with her children and others to the end. She was ambitious for us and encouraged our progress. She gave everything to make us better. My mother made it possible for others to shine and as her daughter I can say that no mother and daughter could have been closer. We were best friends. She literally accompanied her children everywhere whenever possible, from school entrance examinations, to travelling to secondary schools after school holidays, to escorting them to university. She made sure we had everything that was needed for our education: fees, books, uniforms and the right equipment. She got to know almost all of our teachers and was on good terms with them. My mother made all the arrangements so that I could travel to the UK for further studies. I was unaware of all the hard work involved. It was a similar case with my elder brother, George. All the arrangements for his going overseas were initiated and executed by my mother, who eventually arranged for a scholarship so he could finish his medical studies in India.

Maternal grandmother aged 98

2: SCHOOL LIFE AND CHARACTER BUILDING

*　*　*

"Train up a child the way he should go: and
when he is old, he will not depart from it"
Proverbs 26: 6

My mother blossomed at St Monica's Girls' School. Though she missed her family terribly, especially her mother, she believed that she was on a mission and so was determined to make the best of it. The students were housed in dormitories which were named 'Hope', 'Courage', 'Patience' and 'Charity'. It was a very happy time for my mother and she grew in strength and stature. The experience for her was akin to a young bird being released from a cage and set free into the world. Her teachers loved her and her enthusiasm to learn and she loved them in return, especially Miss Ross. My mother was keen to learn and they loved to teach her. She was regularly top of the class in most subjects and was a committed and dedicated student. Apart from academic studies (she loved English most), my mother also excelled in singing, needlework and cookery. Later she passed her knowledge of these skills on to me. This expertise and love of needlework turned out to be very lucky also for one of her granddaughters. One of my daughters wasn't very good at needlework in secondary school and used to bring all her needlework assignments (knitting, crocheting and sewing) home during the school holidays for my mother to complete. My mother loved working on such assignments to help her granddaughter and her needlework was always beautifully completed.

As a young school girl, my mother was very good at sports. She was slender and nimble and her friends would joke that the wind could blow her over when she was sprinting down the tracks. Her friends would chorus "B.U lie down, B.U lie down". "B.U", short for Bernice Uwanugo, was her nickname in school. She still plaited her hair in two, parted down the middle in straight pigtails which reached the base of her neck as her mother used to do. Her physical features gave her the appearance of a beautiful gazelle.

My mother graduated from St Monica's Girls' School in 1931, passing her final exams with flying colours. As much as she wanted to return to Igbodo, the missionaries, especially Miss Ross, wanted her to stay with them a bit longer at Iyienu Hospital near Onitsha to learn more. The idea was for her to stay with them until her marriage, learning more about housekeeping and homebuilding by helping Miss Ross around the home and also helping out at Iyienu hospital. She was given a little weekly allowance. My mother, her parents and her future husband agreed to this Iyienu arrangement and her allowance presented an opportunity to send little gifts, like the local bath soap and clothing to her parents Rachael and Isaiah and younger brother Obed. Mum made the best of every opportunity and used the whole experience as a valuable way to improve her life and the lives of those around her.

One day Rachael (my grandmother) arrived suddenly and unexpectedly to visit my mother at the hospital where she worked. It was a shock and heartbreaking for my mother to see the condition that her mother was in. Her mother had arrived, unannounced, in thread-bare clothes and had walked all the way from Igbodo, a distance of about 30 miles east of the Niger River to visit her daughter. After they had exchanged a few hugs and tears, my mother and her mother shared the little bread she had in her room, then my mother went and bought a four yard piece of "abada cloth"[7], put it round her mother, and gave her three additional pieces of cloth to take home. My mother also went and bought the commonly-used local soap, locally made from palm kernel oil and usually sold in tennis ball sizes. Inside this she hid some coins for her mother to take home. My mother always hid the money she gave her mother, either because she didn't want anyone to know about it or they weren't allowed to send money home. She never really explained to me why this was so.

As previously stated, my father (from the neighbouring town of Owerre-Olubor) was a "pupil teacher" at Igbodo Central School and being a Christian convert himself from an early age, was known to my mother's family. His wish to marry my mother was made known to her family and they agreed. He was the only Christian convert in *his* family and his father couldn't understand it. However, it was a fact that a married woman in our culture at the time and even now to a certain extent, was completely identified with her husband and his people, and this troubled my grandmother. Husbands and their families often had total monopoly of their wives. Would she ever see her daughter as often as she wanted to? Miss Ross got to know my father too and she made my mother's white lace wedding dress

---

[7] Made with cotton, these often-colourful cloths can be tied, one round the chest to reach the ankles or if one had two pieces of material, one piece would first be tied round the waist to reach the ankles and the other tied round the waist to reach the knee.

in the style of Queen Victoria's era. My father described Miss Ross as a little kind lady.

The wedding of my parents on 26th December 1932 was a grand, joyous and an emotional occasion, especially for both mothers of the bride and groom. My mother was a much-wanted only daughter, just as my father was a much-loved only son of her mother and the eldest of his own nuclear family.

It was a white Christian wedding in the style and tradition of the Anglican Church. Sadly my maternal grandfather had passed away the year before.

I'm going to narrate my parents wedding day as passed down to me by my parents:

The wedding took place at 11am on a Saturday morning at St George's CMS (Church Missionary Society) Church, Igbodo. It was "harmattan", the time of year in Nigeria (November to March) when it is usually cold at night and in the mornings but sweltering hot in the afternoons. My mother's wedding dress was made of white lace by Miss Ross. Her hair was in one plait down her back, with a small fringe in front. On top was a short veil made of fine white lace held down by a simple coronet. She wore dangling silver earrings and a long silver necklace, and carried a bouquet of hibiscus flowers and kana lilies. Miss Ross insisted my mother wore stockings with her stylish silver-coloured wedding shoes which had medium heels. My father said my mother looked a dream! My mother said she was nervous on the day but "was looking forward to the next stage of her life."

My father, who was always fashion conscious and loved to dress well, looked impeccable in his Western-style beige suit with a blue and white striped tie and brand new brown shoes to match. "My suit was made at Onitsha and cost a few shillings', my father told me proudly. "I felt quite nervous on my wedding day but knew I had acquired a great prize", he concluded.

As children we were fascinated by my father's pose in their wedding picture. He was standing, with his right hand held akimbo on his right hip, with legs crossed. He informed us that the photographer had asked him to do so in order to look tough! My parents had only two photos taken on their wedding day – one of themselves and one with their parents and important guests. The latter never survived, lost when my parents fled Benin City during the Nigerian / Biafran civil war of 1967.

The church wedding over, the newlyweds and guests walked and sang church hymns all the way through the bush tracks to the reception in my father's home town of Owerre-Olubor, eight miles away. The guests were mainly, friends and family members and the entire church community of Igbodo and Owerre-Olubor. A huge marquee, built of bamboo trunks driven into the ground and roofed with palm fronds to shade the sun had been erected at his father's Owerre-Olubor compound. The seats around the marquee were also made from bamboo trunks. Some chairs and tables were borrowed from the school for the high table and special guests. The place was teeming with people in rich brilliant colours - floral tops and wrappers or "rapas"[8], western clothes and the traditional white local woven cloths known as "ogbenye-apani", usually worn on special occasions by some elders. Many people wore sandals or slippers and others just walked around bare-foot but well-dressed. Dancing groups in different outfits were everywhere: family groups, church groups, the mothers' union, groups of older girls, village groups of friends and same-age groups.

My maternal grandmother, Rachael, was the happiest and proudest mother alive. She cut an amazing figure in her white "ogbenye apani", which was draped round her. Her favourite

---

[8] Made from different fabrics, a wrapper is a traditional garment of West African origin usually worn by women. Although they can also be worn informally, commonly, wrappers are also worn during wedding ceremonies.

song throughout was "Chukwu kam so uzo i" ("Thy way, not mine, oh Lord"). My maternal grandfather would have loved to witness this special and very happy occasion!

Both my grandmothers (Rachael and Ezie) looked magnificent in their best "ogbenye apani." This attire comes in two different sized strips: the bigger one (four yards) is tied round the midriff to reach the ankles and the smaller piece (two yards) is tied round the chest to reach below the knee. Rachael and Ezie, my father's mother, were decked with expensive coral beads round their necks, wrists and ankles. Ezie, being the wife of a chief (Iyase), added her hallmark ankle and wristbands made from elephant tusks. Also in attendance at the wedding was my mother's brother Obed, her uncle Nathaniel, also a Christian convert, and other relatives on both sides of the family. My father's parents were extremely proud of their son too. My paternal grandfather, Kehi, the Iyase of Owerre-Olubor, was swathed in pure white "Ogbenye apani". Like the women, he wore layers of coral beads round his neck and wrists. Chiefs like my paternal grandfather, whose power was supreme in our society, carried 'uyesi' (preserved tail of a dead horse). They waved this slowly and gently in front of their faces from time to time. These were also used to keep flies at bay.

My father's dear and close sister Otubo was very prominent at the wedding too. Otubo and my father were the only two children of their mother (the first wife) though they had other half- siblings, through their father's second marriage. My aunt Otubo was petite, light in complexion with a pretty face like my dad's. She was always happy and giggly. Otubo arranged all her age group's dancing sets. St George's church choir sang their hearts out on the day. My mother's friends and former classmates Jesse Ugbe and Martha Chiazor, (who latter also married a clergyman) were also in attendance.

Many goats and chickens were slaughtered. People offered what they could afford and there were no shortage of cooks. The feast comprised of jollof rice (tomato-based rice) and pounded yam or "yam fufu" swallowed with "egusi" (pumpkin seed) or okra soup. The drink of the day was mainly palm wine, a drink tapped from the top or side of the palm kernel tree into an attached gourd. When freshly drawn, it's very sweet but after some days or weeks, it tastes spirituous in flavour and can intoxicate.

When everyone had settled down and before the feasting commenced, there were speeches by Mr, (later Rev.) Diai in praise of my father and Miss Ross spoke of her beloved pupil, Bernice. While the eating, singing and dancing were in full swing, my parents were fanned with huge fans throughout by enthusiastic relatives. This wedding procession began all the way from the church. Praise singers from both sides of the family showered the young couple with praises. Of my father, they praised, "Nwa Iyase Owelle" (great son of our chief), "Nwa ogbuji" (son of a mighty farmer), "Ejakpukwama ji" (the soil that holds vegetation together), "Nwa mali ekwukwo" (brainy son), "Egbuwei" (no one can harm you) and on and on it went. My mother was praised as "a beautiful "ada oyibo"(modern daughter), the daughter who made her parents and her people proud, the child who brought laughter and joy to her parents, the child of those who brought light and Christianity to Igbodo, a child of hope and good news", and on and on it went. The traditional singers and dancers also wove my parents' names and praises into their songs. There were drums, horns, 'egogos'[9], isia (beaded gourd rattle) and flutes, all deployed in praise of

---

[9] Also called "Ogene", the Egogo is "a type of bell ... it is an instrument of the struck idiophone class and is made of iron by specialist blacksmiths. The bell has a flattish, conical shape, and is hollow inside. The sound itself comes from the vibration of the iron body when struck, which is made to resound by the hollow inside of the bell. The iron body is usually struck with a soft wooden stick." http://en.wikipedia.org/wiki/Ogene [accessed 25th June 2011].

the newlyweds and their ancestors. The newlyweds and dancers were showered with cowries used as coins in those days. The dance styles were mainly indigenous. Dances in Nigeria usually express and evoke situations, emotions, sentiments, and beliefs. Male dancers perform with vigorous jumps and leaps while the women dancers perform bent body postures and bent knee positions. Upper body movements are an essential part of our dance.

"It was an amazing and unforgettable occasion that went on into the early hours of the following morning" my father said. In addition to money gifts from those who could afford it, the wedding presents consisted mainly of cooking utensils – pots, pans and Turin dishes as well as indigenous "abadas" and other clothing materials.

Niger Bridge, Onitsha

Two days later, my exhausted parents returned to my father's teaching post at Ekwuoma, five miles east of Igbodo in the Asaba division. Their mothers and a few close relatives, carrying her wedding presents on bicycles and some on their heads, went with them. My parents dreamed of a big family because my father's mother had two surviving children and my mother's mother also had two surviving children. My parents were blessed with four: George, Samuel (lost tragically at the age of five), Grace (myself) and Patrick. It is sad for me that I never knew my paternal grandparents. Ezie, my grandmother, died fairly young in 1934 of strangulated hernia and Kehi, my grandfather, died in 1940 of heart failure. In another sense, I feel I know them from all I have been told about them.

3: MY FATHER – ARCHDEACON GABRIEL IKEDUBA KERRY

* * *

"Be the change you wish to see in the world."
Mahatma Gandhi (1869 - 1948)

My father was named IKEDUBA (there is strength in numbers) at birth.

The history of my mother's life is intertwined with that of my father. He was her rock and her best friend and their lives were joined in true friendship. It is difficult to separate the two lives. Proverbs 8:22 states that, "he who finds a (good) wife finds a good thing and obtains favour from the Lord." My father found not only a wife but a treasure of a wife, who truly loved him and whom he truly loved. Personality-wise, my parents were opposites and both could be determined but it worked very well for them. In truth my father merits a book about his own life which was just as remarkable as that of my mother.

My father was born in Owerre-Olubor, a small tropical town eight miles from Igbodo, in Western Nigeria as it was then known. He was strikingly good-looking and as a young boy stood out in school and in the community. As a child, people often mistook him for a little girl because he looked girly and he was nicknamed "Ikeduba-okpoho" (Ikeduba girl). He was also teased with "Baba oge-akwukwo elue" ('Dad, it's time for school") because he loved school and that was what he used to say to his father when he heard the school gong. He dropped everything at the sound of the school bell! My father started school at about the age of ten (his actual date of birth is unknown) loved learning and did exceptionally well at school. He attended various primary schools around his area, which were, the CMS Schools in Owerre-Olubor, Akwukwu-Akumazi (now Ekwuoma) and Igbodo and finally, Ubulu-Ukwu Central School where he passed the government Standard Six (primary school leaving) examination in 1928. These fledgling schools only had one or two class levels and pupils moved to a different school for the next level(s). The next stage of my father's education was at CMS Training College in Obosi near Onitsha in 1930 before he got married. From 1936 to 1937, he attended CMS Training College Awka, as a trainee catechist. He practised as a catechist and schoolteacher until 1955 when he was ordained as a Deacon by Rt. Rev. Oyebode, Assistant Bishop of Ondo / Benin Diocese.

This achievement made my parents, particularly my father, very happy, because he knew that the next step after that would be the ordination into full priesthood which was his lifelong ambition. His dream came true in Ondo Cathedral on 16th December 1956, and the ceremony was performed by Rev. Odutola, Bishop of Ondo / Benin Diocese. My father's generation of clergymen were true men of God, they were gems, who served God with absolute dedication and sincerity, initiating positive changes in the world. They fought the good fight and never wanted for themselves. They were not grasping like many clergymen (from different denominations) of today. My parents' times are long gone.

Wedding – December 1932

Now, false prophets abound! Many religious leaders in Nigeria today fleece and milk their parishioners for all they can get and strip their congregation of the little they possess. As soon as many people assume religious leadership, they want big cars, big houses and as many worldly possessions they could squeeze from their parishioners. It's "gimme gimme gimme". The poorest parishioners suffer the most. Every Sunday, it starts with an announcement, and the clergyman prancing around – "If it's your birthday or that of any family member come for thanks-giving." Then people dance up the aisle to give what they have. The next announcement goes, "this is the first Sunday of the month, please give." This is accompanied by more singing and dancing and offerings, followed by, "please give more for being alive." Then, "come and be 'healed'." On and on it goes. All this performed with Biblical theatricality and Sunday services drag on forever! At the end of the services, off the men and women trot home to gather more for the "church". The "men of God" definitely show no mercy, sympathy or empathy for their flock. Worst of all, the parishioners secrets are definitely no longer safe with many clergymen.

Invite them into your home and they tell the world how you live. They tell it as they see and hear it! Most of the clergy, starting from the catechist want to be Archdeacons and Bishops and Primates as soon as possible and their congregation come second. The name of God is bandied in vain! There is a proliferation of all kinds of churches in Nigeria today. This is not to mock those who do some marvellous work in the church but there are also many false 'prophets!'

As my father progressed up the ecumenical ladder, his ministerial activities continued to diversify. There were a few detractors along the way but most parishioners loved my father's work and were often mesmerised by his warmth, charisma and power of preaching. He had such compassion that sometimes, conducting funerals, he would be overcome by emotion. Before he trained as a church catechist, he taught as a primary school teacher and school master in various places, including the CMS School in Onu-iyi Ogbahu in the Asaba

District; Orogodo in the Agbor district; Isele-Azagba in Asaba District; Akwu-kwu Akumazi, (now Ekwuoma) in the Asaba District and Onitsha-Ugbo in the Asaba district. In many of these posts, my father acted as an Ibo and Yoruba (two of the three Nigerian main languages) interpreter during church services. He spoke the two languages fluently, as well as fluent English.[10]

As children, we were very touched when my father told us the length that his mother, Ezie went to in order to make sure he was well-fed at the beginning of his teaching career. His mother would cook a few days' quantity of jollof rice and pounded yam ("fufu") with "egusi" soup, which was my father's favourite food. His sister Otubo and their female cousin, Ohu would carry these bowls of food in huge gourd containers (hollowed out and dried and used to store things) on their heads, all the way, eight miles, on foot to his first teaching post in Iselle-Azagba! After all, he was his mother's adored only son.

From early to mid 1940s, my father served as a catechist at a number of churches in Eastern Nigeria, namely at Mbu Amon in the Nsukka District, Eha Amufu in Nsukka District and as catechist and group leader at Umunze. In 1943, my parents were transferred to Bishop Tugwell Memorial (BTM) Church in Lagos. From Lagos, they were transferred to CMS Church, Abraka, in 1946, then onto Christ Church, Obiarukwu in 1948 and St John's Church Abbi, in 1950 – all in the Kwale District of the then Mid-Western Nigeria. My father's transfer to St Paul's Ibo Church, Benin City, in 1951 opened many avenues for our family, because to begin with, he was ordained there as a priest in 1955 and was made superintendent of all Ibo churches in the Benin

---

[10] Whilst there are over one hundred and fifty tribes in the country, Nigeria has three main languages. "Igbo" is spoken predominantly in the east of the country, "Yoruba" is spoken in the west and "Hausa" is spoken in the north of Nigeria, with many more dialects spoken within each language.

conurbation. Our home was always heaving with people both young and old – friends, relatives, cousins, nephews, nieces, children of family friends and young engaged girls whose husbands-to-be wanted them to learn home-making tips from my mother. Many lived with us. My parents welcomed them all with open arms, and nurtured and supported their education.

My father was a great storyteller, with a sense of drama. As children he would sit us round him on Friday evenings and tell us amazing tales and fables, such as the tale of the slow but crafty tortoise who would always cheat on everybody including his wife and children. We also learnt why the man in the full moon was fixed there "breaking fire-wood". He was punished for breaking wood on a Sunday. We learned why the baby deer was left an orphan-his mother disregarded his plea to go home. Papa told us of the picky young girl in search of a husband who fell for a python in human form. The man returned into his original state as a reptile after they were married and swallowed up his wife. There were many such fables my father told us. He would dramatise the animals' gestures and movements, and the way they walked and 'talked'. He also taught us the various songs that went with the tales. Occasionally my mother would join in the fun. When we cheered and clapped at the end of it all, my father would smile his lovely smile and laugh too, showing the small gap in the centre of his perfectly formed upper front teeth. He taught us to sing all the verses of "Who Killed Cock Robin?" My father did not have the perfect singing voice but he didn't mind and would sing with gusto all the same.

He would sing the first verse: "Who killed Cock Robin?" "I", said the sparrow, "With my bow and arrow. I killed Cock Robin". At this stage, my father would gesture "join" and we all joined in till the last verse, when he would again sing alone, feigning sorrow, "All the birds of the air, Fell a-sighing and a-sobbing, when they heard the bell toll, for poor Cock Robin".

Sometimes we asked for a repeat performance and my father would oblige. Our childhood was simple and basic but joyous. I loved and still love my dad very much. He was a wonderful father to me.

My father called us to family prayers every morning and night with a hand-bell. Prayers were essential in our lives and said every morning at 6am and 9pm before bed. This involved Bible reading, hymn singing and a prayer said by my father or my mother, if she was home. My father particularly loved the rendition of his favourite hymn, "To God Be the Glory Great Things, He Hath Done". His deep voice would rise to a crescendo at the chorus, 'Praise the Lord, Praise the Lord, Let the people rejoice". As we grew older we took it in turns to read the Bible passages during prayers.

My father – Benin City, 1962

My family also said regular grace before and after meals. Breakfast was usually "akamu" (our local custard made of corn starch) and "akara" (this is fried black-eyed beans flour paste). Schools usually started in Nigeria at 8.30pm and closed at 2pm and we always walked to and from school, a distance of about four miles return. I attended the prestigious CMS Girls' primary school, Benin City and my younger brother attended St James' (mixed) Primary School, Benin City. Though we had school sandals, my friends and I from school would sometimes walk home bare-foot, our sandals in our school bags, especially in the dry season (October - May) so we could feel the heat of the hot grass or sand on the soles of our feet. This was a childhood game of who could tolerate the heat better. Dinner at home was usually rice or "fufu" with okra or egusi soup or boiled yam with tomato and meat stew. Any homework had to be finished before 8pm.

There were street taps in Benin City but not in our house or compound, so, if there was no water in our huge water drums at the back of the house, we (the children in the house) would fetch water with buckets from the street taps to fill them up before evening prayers. We were very happy and excited when taps were later installed in our vicarage after two years in Benin City. Fetching water from street taps was no joke! There was usually a long line (or rather a crowd) of anxious men, women and children with buckets and basins waiting for their turn to get water but nobody ever took any notice of queues. It was the law of the jungle and there were regular fights! The young and weak suffered the most. The strongest battered the children aside and jumped the queue and the wait was usually long. Sometimes we got into fights and my father would be sent for to collect us home. I did not see it as hardship though, because most people were affected in the same way.

My father was a bit more reserved and more cautious than my mother. He was clever, funny, articulate and softly-spoken. My parents were opposite personalities that gelled and though they could both be strong-willed, one often gave in to the other because they found great companionship with one another. My mother was fearless, highly intelligent, vibrant, very articulate and outspoken. My father was more reserved.

Due to the fact that my father was born into a farming community and was one of the handful of people from Owerre-Olubor at that time to attend school (something that benefitted the town and his people), there was no record of his birth. He was always keen to keep records because of this omission in his life. He kept the records of all the births, marriages and deaths for all of his family and friends, to make up for the lack of the record of his own birth and those of family members before him. Record-keeping was very important to him. Throughout his missionary career, he kept what he called a "ledger" of all his experiences, happy or sad, pleasant and unpleasant alike. Unfortunately, this "treasure" left to my mother, disappeared after my mother died. Someone must have stolen it and probably destroyed it. My father also loved and served his native Owerre-Olubor well. Until the early forties Owerre-Olubor was known as Owerre-Akumazi. It was subordinated to Akumazi, the neighbouring village but my father spear-headed the campaign for Owerre-Olubor's autonomy which was eventually granted in the mid 70s and the town became officially known as Owerre-Olubor as it is today.

My father strongly believed that he had a vocation to serve God. The great urge and calling to go to school in the first place was the precursor to this. Every vocation or calling requires certain physical and mental attributes and talents, and only those blessed with the right attributes can achieve success in their chosen profession. The Church in particular and religious ministry in general, requires high standards of morality and educational training as well as a practical awareness and knowledge of the world. Those called to the service of God, should possess integrity, honesty, love, patience and a willing heart to serve God for very little or no reward; qualities hard to find in many clergymen and women today. A clergyman must also be devout, empathetic, sympathetic, honest, cheerful and pleasant. Those were the outstanding qualities possessed by my father, which guided him in the successful execution of his global church ministry.

Papa (as we called him) always believed or guessed he was probably born around the same year (1904) as Dr Nnamdi Azikiwe ("Zik of Africa"), the first President of Nigeria and the man who led Nigeria to independence in 1960. This was only a strong hunch and there was no evidence for this assumption. In those days, however, people often linked momentous personal events (births, marriages and deaths) with landmark events both locally and in the wider world, such as the arrival of the missionaries, the World Wars, the influenza epidemic of the First World War, the salt scarcity and locust infestations of the war years when my parents were based in Eastern Nigeria.

My father hated working on the farm from childhood, which disappointed his father, a renowned farmer and the "Iyase" (ruler / Chief) of Owerre Olubor. Looking at my father and knowing him, he didn't look like he belonged to the farming community. His skin was soft and beautiful like a girl's. With his excellent mind, he was destined for academic life. His father's first name was Kehi, later changed to Keri, then Kerry. His father's surname was Ugbe. My father's mother, Ezie (from the neighbouring village of Ute-Ogbeje) was of noble birth herself. People always described her as very fair or light in complexion, extremely beautiful, very fresh-looking and always well-presented with her customary elephant tusk bands round her wrists and ankles. My paternal grandfather was often described as a handsome big man with a big heart. My father inherited both of his parents' features. It was a disappointment to Kehi, when his first son chose school above farming, because, apart from anything else, my father was the only son of his mother (the first of his father's two wives) and the eldest child of the family. A farming community needed strong young men but my father, though strong, was determined to go to school and pursue his education.

In 1920, my father was baptised "Gabriel Ikeduba" and later became a "pupil teacher", that is, a primary school teacher. It was his mentor Mr Diai (later ordained a pastor in the Anglican Church) who started calling my father "Keri" instead of "Kehi" because Mr Diai's dialect had no "h" sound.

After his christening, my father felt he was called to come over to the Lord's vineyard to work for The Lord. He made history as the first Ibo pastor to be ordained as a priest in the old Ondo / Benin Diocese of Nigeria, and was also the sole vicar and superintendent of the Ibo churches in the Benin conurbation. Moreover, he served on the District Church Council Board and Synod meetings. Additionally, he was the prison and leper settlement chaplain in Benin City for many years. Owerre-Olubor Patriotic Union was founded by my father and he was its first President. My father loved his people and St Barnabas Church, Owerre-Olubor, which he supported all his life. He worked relentlessly and whole-heartedly throughout his life for his people and the church.

My father was an excellent and influential teacher, and so his pupils always remembered him. One of his old pupils paid for a brand new car engine for him in 1976 when his old car engine packed up. This was no mean feat in those days but this former student never forgot the influence my father had in his life because selflessly, my father helped others to rise and encouraged them to fulfil their true potential.

Hard work and intellectual rigor were important virtues in the eyes of my father and both my parents worked very hard together to give their children the best education possible. My elder brother George (now deceased) was a qualified medical doctor, I have a doctorate degree in Education and my younger brother Patrick is a barrister.

Having witnessed her parents' unhappy marriage, my mother vowed to build a loving home for her husband and children, and so, it came to pass.

This is for my father as written by Swiss composer Paul Burkhard:

Oh my papa, to me he was so wonderful
Oh my papa, to me he was so good
No one could be so gentle and so lovable
Oh my papa, He always understood
Gone are the days when he would take me on his knee
And with a smile, He'd change my tears to laughter
Oh, my papa, to me he was so wonderful
Deep in my heart, I miss him so today
Oh my papa!

4: MISSIONARY JOURNEYS AND FAMILY LIFE

* * *

"If your actions inspire others to dream more, learn more, do more or become more, you are a leader."
John Quincy Adams, 6th President of the United States, (1767-1848)

After their wedding in December 1932, my parents were posted to Ekwuoma, about five miles east of my father's village. My eldest brother was born there. My parents had four children between 1933 and 1942, three sons and one daughter. Their first son George was born at Ekwuoma followed by Samuel, then Grace and Patrick. My mother continued to support her husband and also cared for young women and brides-to-be, teaching them to cook, crotchet, knit, sew and also the word of God. My mother was a born leader: self-assured, assertive, dynamic, hardworking, compassionate, and an accomplished cook. Her style was always to lead by example. One of my mother's protégés often gave testimony of how my mother would teach the young girls who lived with her to prepare various meals well into the night. She never went off to bed and left the girls to finish off the cooking or clear up the kitchen. Instead she stayed

with them until the food was cooked to perfection and made sure
everything was packed away and tidied up before going to bed herself. My mother made hard work look easy! I remember how my mother would often stay up late on Christmas Eve, well after midnight, making dresses for me and my cousin, Rosa, who lived with us, so we could wear brand new dresses to church on Christmas day.

Lagos 1944

My parents were transferred to Issele Azagba in 1936, from where my father was sent to Akwa College on the first leg of his training for vocational church work. My mother was still working very hard as a teacher's wife and looking after her own two young sons. It was at this stage that her mother offered to take the eldest boy, George to Igbodo while my mother looked after the younger son, Samuel. This was a fairly common practice in the Nigerian culture; grandmothers sharing the up-bringing of their grandchildren.

My mother was overjoyed because she needed support and she and her mother were very close. So it came about that my elder brother George went to live with my grandmother until my father finished his training. My grandmother was a very loving, very spiritual and very religious person, as well as having great physical strength, even in her old age. She moved in with my parents for the last fifteen years of her long life of one hundred and two years. Even at that great age she would porter round the garden picking fruits or weeding grass.

My grandmother's praying sessions were marathons and legendary. She could kneel (even on an arthritic knee) for up to an hour at a time in prayers. If we were staying with her during some Easter or Christmas holidays, as my parents made sure we did, we were always called to prayers first thing in the morning, around 5pm (cock's crow) and last thing at night (around 8 or 9 pm) except when the moon was shining, when we would sit round and listen to my granny's fables.) My granny had no clock, and people often rose very early to go the farms. Some farms were near home and some were miles away. Home farms, about a mile away, were small farms where people grew simple crops like vegetables, pepper, onions, maize, okra etc and where they could pop in and out quickly. Large farms, where large-scale farming (of yam and cassava) and animal hunting took place, were about six to seven miles away through thick forest. During my granny's long prayers, most of the family members present, who sometimes visited, would leave by the end of her prayers. We children never did. We knelt till the end of her long prayers, though some of us might dose off kneeling down . She would mention her children and grandchildren by the names she gave them, one by one, commending them all to the care of God. Her love and devotion were evident daily and her prayers have always followed us and clung to us all our lives! My granny also loved her clay pipe. She and her friends would sit around after our family evening prayers and enjoy a smoke and my mother usually bought her the best tobacco!

My father finished his vocational training in 1937 and rejoined his family. My parents were then transferred to a village called Ihamufu in Eastern Nigeria. This was a remote and dangerous territory, where wild cats such as lions, tigers and cheetahs came out of their lairs at night in search of food. They prowled, purred and roared around the villages and houses. The nights were dangerous. Once darkness fell, people locked themselves indoors. My parents were never afraid because they were steadfast in their work and faith.

Nsukka, now a university town in Eastern Nigeria, was where my parents worked from 1940 – 1943. They were often posted from village to village to support and supervise fledgling churches and primary schools. The year 1942 was a tragic year for the family. My older brother Samuel died in a fire tragedy on Christmas day. The two older boys were playing outside in the front garden, three days before Christmas. No one knew exactly what happened but suddenly there was a heart-rending scream. My mother was not very well and was in bed. My father ran out to check what was happening and was confronted by a terrible spectacle. Their beautiful boy was ablaze! My father ripped off Sam's shirt but it was too late. My older brother Sam (as he was affectionately called), a much loved son and brother, was rushed to Iyienu General Hospital, near Onitsha about 40 miles away.

He died on Christmas day, 1942, aged five. The trauma of that loss lingered over my family for a very long time.

My mother had a sort of premonition about Sam but never imagined a catastrophe of such magnitude. She was enveloped in grief and deeply mourned her lost boy! She fled to Igbodo with her three remaining children to be cared for by her mother.

Mum, dad and me 1946

My grandmother though bereft with grief herself saved her daughter's life. My father was also grief-stricken beyond description because he had already experienced the loss of his dear father earlier in the year.

"I was disorientated with sorrow and couldn't walk for days," my Mum remembered, "my whole body fell apart. I lost all strength and nearly fell off the boat into the River Niger, travelling from Iyi-Enu hospital to Igbodo". The shock of losing her beautiful baby was so profound and all-encompassing that for the rest of her life, my mother barely talked about him. Very occasionally, she would mention his passing but never in detail. Once she said the missionaries used to say to her that "Samuel looks more like you than your other children" and how Sam once ran home at that young age to tell her, (my mother) that one of the church workers was giving him an evil eye.

The Second World War was raging when my parents were transferred in 1944 to Bishop Tugwell Memorial (BTM) Church, Lagos, which was the chief commercial centre of Nigeria at that time. BTM church was a huge church for the Ibo speaking congregation in Lagos. The train journey from Nsukka to Lagos was long and arduous and was made even more difficult with three young children. Settled in Lagos, my mother was being increasingly recognised for her leadership qualities. The Second World War was in full swing and food was scarce but we had all the love and comfort we needed. The War reduced the British Government's imports, investment and Government spending in Nigeria. Subsequently, the British government assumed total control of the local economy in Nigeria. It only issued trade licenses to established firms and this formalised the competitive advantage of foreign companies. Wartime marketing boards fixed the prices of food items below the world market rate. This meant that workers encountered wage ceilings which were frozen, consumers experienced shortages of imported goods and local traders encountered price controls. Thus the "Control Market" in Lagos was born.

The Second World War years were eventful for my mother. She was one of those selected by the government to act as one of the agents for the "Control Market", which involved selling locally-grown produce to the public. These were usually food items, bought at a fixed rate and sold to the traders and civilians at a little profit. My family benefitted from this venture because we had a lot to eat – seafood, pork meat, beef, and a variety of vegetables, rice, yams, plantain, black-eyed beans and more. I remember my mother coming home once with a bag full of huge crabs. She emptied them into a big basin and they started to crawl all over the place. My brothers and I ran amok with shock, screaming! We had never seen crabs nor eaten them before, but when cooked, they were actually delicious!

The "Control Market" was an elitist system and was not accessible to all who wanted to be part of it. My mother obviously got into it because of my father's status and her own enterprising efforts.

A major episode in Lagos during this period was the day that we thought my younger brother Patrick, aged three, was lost or stolen. On this particular day, my parents came home and he wasn't there. They checked at their family friends, (the Onughas) home, but he wasn't there either. They rushed around the neighbourhood desperately searching for him and shouting his name. All the neighbours joined in because there were no emergency services to alert. My parents rushed back home despairing and screaming. When they got home my mother's wailing woke Patrick, who scrambled out from under the bed where he was sleeping, screaming in fear because of the din around him. What happened was that my parents were away and he had been threatened with a beating by a neighbour known as "mama ogi"; so called, because she sold ogi, a kind of gruel made from corn powder served for breakfast. So Patrick hid under the bed and fell fast asleep, until my mother's screams woke him up. My mother was understandably deeply distressed at the thought of losing another child, not long after the fire tragedy which claimed Sam's life. My parents' relief at finding my baby brother safe and well was indescribable. From then on, they kept a close watch on my brother who was very precocious, inquisitive and mischievous. He was always so very curious and keen to investigate things like most children his age and said what he thought and felt. It was fairly common when we were growing up, for children to stay with neighbours if their parents weren't around and it was common practice for friendly mothers to feed or look after friendly neighbours' children. However, we were never left with neighbours because my mother's cousin Janet was always at home with us. Patrick was a very pretty child and people liked him a lot and would invite him to their homes to play with their children, a practice my parents never encouraged. There was another worrying incident in my family shortly after, concerning my younger brother. He developed a raw-looking and swollen abscess on his chin. My mother was very concerned about this and she invited a local nurse, Noel, to examine it and advice. After close inspection, the nurse promised to return the following day to lance the boil. After he left, my mother couldn't bear the thought of a scar being left on her beautiful baby's chin, so she took matters into her own hands. She would lance the boil with the prick of a needle, thereby leaving a minimal scar. It worked! When Noel came back the following day, my mother told him the boil had burst by itself. Patrick, however, told the nurse exactly what had happened, which left my parents very embarrassed! The good bit was that the matter of the boil was resolved without any huge drama and Noel saw the funny side as well.

In fact, my mother was adept at self and home medication. Her mother knew a lot about local herbs but my mother went further. If any of the children has a wound or cut that was not healing, my mother would pick a lime fruit, cut it in half, squeeze out the beeps, sprinkle the surface of the wound with the lime juice, then use the cut surface to clean the wound,

Village gathering 1953 with my parents and my
maternal grandmother on the right of my father

rubbing round it. When the face of the wound is clean, she would crush a tablet resembling codeine tablet called "M&B" (a kind of antibiotics manufactured by the pharmaceutical, May and Baker) with some yellow granules, called ogwu-edo (yellow medicine). The powder is then sprinkled on the wound. The wound healed in days! If anyone had what was suspected to be malaria fever, my mother knew effective herbs and leaves for the cure.

The appropriate medicinal ingredients were gathered and boiled with water in a big pot. It cooked for an hour and the sick child would be bathed in the cooled water from the pot. Some of the medicinal liquid of the boiled leaves is bottled and drunk over a few days. This was a very effective cure for malaria! If any child had ring warms on their head, my mother knew a potent pungent smelling plant called "ubulutu" which she used to banish the agony of ringworms. First she would shave the child's head, then collect the tender leaves at the top end of the plant, wilt them a little, extract the liquid, and treat the scalp with it.

Children walked barefoot almost all the time in those days so we sometimes got thorns or wood splinters lodged into the soles of our feet. My mother would soak the foot twice a day in hot water for three days until the thorn pulled out. My mother was also a dab hand at extracting jiggers with sewing needles from the sole of children's feet. Jiggers are tropical sand fleas that burrow and lay eggs beneath the skin, mainly the feet. They cause itching, swelling and infection. The young jiggers or larva hatches from the eggs which feed on man. Once the larva is removed the wound is sealed with a dab of iodine.

The bishops and senior clergy trusted my parents totally and my mother was always called upon to organise huge meetings and gatherings such as the Synod, church rallies and inter-church conferences, all of which she carried out effectively. She loved to cook and was perfect at organising and mobilising women for good work, both socially and in the church. Moreover, she was very knowledgeable and had the kind of natural authority which people believed in and trusted. She taught mothers how to look after their children and families and how to be good supportive wives. Husbands left their future wives with my mother for months before their weddings, to be schooled in the Christian way and my mother played her role to perfection. She encouraged the brides-to-be to speak properly, to stand tall, to eat properly and to care for their looks.

My father was always proud of my mother, though at times he worried in case her business ventures impacted negatively on his position as a clergyman. Some people frowned on a clergyman's wife carrying on with business activities instead of focussing on her church work and some were openly malicious and critical, spreading false gossips.

However, my parents thrived in Lagos, though financially, life was still tough due to the effects of the Second World War. Even amongst the members of my father's congregation, there were a few scheming, back-biting and back-stabbing individuals to contend with. My father was often hurt by these

Diocesan meeting in 1960

actions and recorded it all in his ledger. He couldn't understand why some members of the congregation displayed signs of spite and hostility towards him and his family. The only possible reason he could think of was, perhaps they were jealous he had three beautiful children and a very capable, beautiful wife who was admired by many. However, the positive experiences he had as a clergyman out-numbered the negative ones which were also recorded in the ledger, such as the births of his children, christenings, his promotions, transfers, examinations passed and compliments about his wife and work.

A clergyman's salary was however very meagre and sometimes there was not enough money to purchase food, let alone proper Sunday clothes for children. What my father didn't have my mother made up. We had free accommodation near the church, paid for by the church and that helped. As very young children, we each had only one Sunday best. During the period when things were really hard, my elder brother George sometimes robed with the choristers on Sundays in only his underpants. My mother was mortified when she heard one of the choir boys sneering at my brother, "why do you wear only your pants to church?" To rectify this embarrassing situation, my mother worked even harder. She improvised all the time, making all my clothes herself and growing vegetables and food crops, both for sale, to supplement the family income and for family consumption.

As children, we were very happy in Lagos. We were content with what we had because we were loved and well looked after. We learnt to speak and write the Yoruba language in school. We lived in the city but near the church. In early years in primary school we were taught the song, "There was an old woman who lived in a shoe" in the Yoruba language and I can still sing it fluently in that language after all those years. Towards the end of the war we were regularly shown a film in school about a massive formidable bear and a huge python. Churchill was depicted as the massive formidable bear and Hitler, the huge long slimy python. The two animals would be shown on screen fighting viciously for a long period until the bear killed the snake, biting into its head and dragging it off the stage in its mouth. They showed this film to school-children time and time again during the war until the end of the war. As an infant school-child it used to scare me because I took it at face value. Later my father explained the moral behind the film; that Prime Minister Churchill (British Empire) being more powerful, triumphed over Hitler (Dictator of Nazi Germany) who wanted to dominate the world. In a way good overcame evil.

My father was a doting dad to me but strict with my brothers and all other children living with us who did not pull their weight. My father believed I was the reincarnation of his mother, Ezie, because as a baby I was the spitting image of her. Whenever he was away on church tours, he always brought back some presents for me (never mind the others), such as a scarf or a basket of oranges or he ordered a sack of rice which was my favourite food. When I passed my West Africa School Certificate Examination (GCSE equivalent) in 1958, my father was so proud of me that he bought me a Raleigh bicycle which was quite something in those days! It came in handy because it made easy travelling to my new job as a teacher in a secondary modern school in Benin, where we lived. I was proud to learn to ride a bicycle and it gave me some independence. Patrick resembled my father physically. Patrick was taller and a good sportsman, especially at football, while George physically resembled my mother. George was very sporty too and developed the elegant bouncing walk of an athlete. My mother was more indulgent towards us than our father was and to her our comfort came first. She was more patient with our misdemeanour than our father who couldn't tolerate indolence or untidiness in anyway especially in our school work.

My parents were posted, in 1946, to a remote town called Abraka in Kwale District (now in Delta State) of what was then Western Nigeria. Today, Abraka is a thriving university town. We lived in a similar house to the ones we had in eastern Nigeria. It was a brick house with corrugated iron sheets, usually with four bedrooms (two on each side) and a parlour in the centre with a veranda in front. The kitchen was a small outhouse at the back, like many kitchens at that time.

We cooked with firewood. Water was fetched from the wells or the very fast-flowing dangerous river Ethiope (whichever was nearer) by the older boys and girls in the house. Sometimes I went with them and had a dip in the river though we were strictly forbidden to do so by my parents because River Ethiope regularly claimed the lives of children who went to swim in it.

My mother worked harder than ever in this rural town. She involved herself in farming because as the catechist, my father had been given a house which, though humble, was surrounded by a huge piece of land. My mother farmed and sold anything that could be farmed: okra, tomatoes, yams, cassava, chickens, goats, pigs, fresh and smoked fish and even tortoises. She hired labourers to help with the work, with sowing, harvesting and with the sale of her produce.

I would say she was a born entrepreneur. She enjoyed doing all of this work and she made it look effortless. Guinea fowls roamed wild and their eggs littered our backyard. It was during these years of growing up that my mother taught me things that I carry with me to this day, such as discipline, compassion, hard work and love of cooking.

She never stopped organising women and teaching different crafts. Her time was also filled with running prayer meetings, attending church meetings and most important of all, telling the truth at all times. She confronted issues head-on. Organising and running women's activities in the church, was firmly the job of the clergymen's wives in those days. She counselled husbands as well.

If a husband failed his wife, Mrs Kerry made it plain that this was not acceptable. If a wife erred, Mrs Kerry made it known to her as well and encouraged her to do better. If children fell foul of good behaviour, Mrs Kerry advised their parents and suggested a probable right course of action.

Senators with dad, far left and mum centre left

Mischief and jealousies continued unabated in different forms during my parents' professional lives. My father often travelled to surrounding villages to visit local churches as part of his parochial duties and also to attend meetings which sometimes lasted two to three days away from home. During these absences, we were usually home with my mother and one or two relatives, usually young female adult cousins.

One particular week in 1947 was quite alarming for my family! Something strange began to happen while my father was away. Every night around midnight someone or something would come to knock three times on our front door and then sprint away as my mother answered the door. These were three loud knocks! The nights were usually pitch-black, except the moon was shining. There was no electricity, so lanterns, hurricane lamps or oil lamps were used in the homes and left on all night. These knocks were frightening and intimidating even for my mother. On the third night, though still scared, my mother bravely decided to get to the bottom of the problem. She grabbed the small hurricane lamp which was always lit at night, woke my older cousin, Faith and waited behind the door for the dreaded knock. The knock came slowly and deliberately three times as usual. My mother moved slowly to open the door. As the door was being opened, someone or something fled. My mother could see the profile of a person as the object sprinted away. Determined to solve the problem once and for all, she stepped outside with the lamp. As she opened the door wide, she could see the silhouette of a man in shorts. She pursued him for a hundred yards as he fled through the wooden rickety gate. Then she stopped as it flashed through her mind to look for footprints. She knew there must be footprints on the dry sandy soil between the front door and the gate. Lo and behold, she saw the footprints, human footprints but the right foot had only three toes. My mother picked up a long stick and circled a few of these footprints as an exhibit or evidence for the parishioners to view the evidence of our midnight tormentor during my father's absence. So, the mystery was cracked through my mother's bravery. My family and the entire community then knew who was terrifying us at night! It was my father's gangly middle-aged church warden, Opia! This man had a deformed right foot with only three toes. It was an almost unbelievable story! The man did not deny what he had done when he was confronted by the church. He begged for forgiveness, saying he only wanted to intimidate us and meant no harm. He was, however, stripped of his position as a church warden and he subsequently left the church.

In the same year a remarkable and extraordinary event took place. The eclipse of the sun! For us and indeed for everyone it was a sudden terrifying experience because we had never known anything like it before, so, did not know what was happening. It felt like we were at the brink of a major cataclysm! My father was away visiting parishioners when this phenomenon started to unfold. All of a sudden, night began to fall in the middle of the day! My mother couldn't make out what was happening either, as the darkness thickened into midnight. The animals became agitated; the chickens were clucking, the birds chirping in a manic way, our little dog was barking, the goats and sheep were bleating. We could hear wailing from the house across the street. Even my brave and clever mother was in a panic but gathered us all together under the bed as if that would protect us from some impending annihilation. Then everything went quiet. My mother started to recite the Lord's Prayer. All the children were crying, including me. We could hear some Jehovah's Witnesses bellowing death and damnation, "The world is at an end, doomsday is here, the end of the world has come, repent, repent, repent, Armageddon is here."

Then, gradually, after what seemed like eternity, the darkness began to clear until the sun reappeared and it was daylight again! My mother began to sing and dance and we all joined in, so happy that we were all still alive. But where was my father? Suddenly, when it was all over, my father walked in, having been marooned on his bicycle on his way home from his usual visits to parishioners due to what we later learned was the eclipse of the sun! The eclipse of the sun is when the Moon passes between the Sun and the Earth and the Moon totally or partially covers the Sun. As this phenomenon was taking place my father had dismounted from his bicycle and sat on the ground beside it, literally waiting for "he didn't know what", until suddenly, the darkness turned to day again. Although my father had suspected what was happening, he was not sure. He had read of eclipses at Teachers' College but had never experienced a total eclipse before. The joy in the household when my father walked in was palpable! We all rushed at him, flung our arms around him all at once laughing and shouting "papa nnua" (welcome papa) and he was hugging us tight.

In 1948, my parents were transferred to another town called Obiarukwu still in the Kwale District of Nigeria. My mother never complained about all of these moves, because she used every opportunity to the best advantage. She loved life and she loved meeting people. She explored the areas, meeting the women, travelling and selling produce like "garri" (grated fried cassava), yams and other crops that she had grown herself and harvested with the help of hired hands. The mountains of garri which she had purchased would be heaped into sacks ready for transportation for sale in big cities like Lagos, Ibadan or Lokoja in Northern Nigeria. It is true my mother was on the move all the time, her life truly revolved round her family and her community. As children we enjoyed the excitement of the regular transfers but it did affect us in one negative way. We couldn't forge lasting friendships in our younger years and as my elder brother George progressed in his primary school education, he was sent to live with my mother's cousin, Steve, in the big town of Warri in the Niger Delta, so he could finish the last year of his primary education, which was Standard six. At that level, children sat the secondary school entrance examination. George lived with Steve, his wife and children for a period of one year but was very homesick.

We lived in Obiarukwu for the next two years, from 1948 - 49. One night in 1949, we were burgled! You can imagine the poverty of the local people, for ordinary church people like us to be burgled. However, my parents didn't realise there were intruders in the house that night, when suddenly, my mother began to scream in pain, apparently because she had been stung by a scorpion. Her screams woke everybody in the house. After she was attended to and her sting was treated with my father's "Igbobi", a local medication, especially prepared as an antidote for poison from dangerous snakes like vipers and scorpion bites. This potion was handed down to my father by his father. My father was a stickler for time-keeping, so, he decided to check the clock for the precise time at which the whole house was woken by my mother's screams but our clock, usually on top of the cupboard in the parlour was gone. While my father was looking around for it in case he had absent-mindedly put it somewhere else during the day, he saw many other household bits and pieces (cutlery, cups, plates, clothes, even foodstuffs) strewn all over the parlour and spilling into the front yard. Then, he realised that we had been burgled and the thieves had fled when they heard my mother's screams. They feared they had been spotted and had dropped all they had stolen as they fled. My father said a thankful prayer to God and we all went back to bed. My mother gradually recovered from her ordeal. The intruders were never caught. Many similar incidents littered my parents' missionary journey, where the poor were so poor that they robbed churchmen.

We were on the move again in 1950. My parents were transferred to another little town, Abbi, about fifteen miles east of Obiarukwu. We were there for the next year. The amazing thing is that the more my parents were sent to far-flung places, the more they thrived and prospered. We were the elite, because my father was a church and school teacher and my mother was also a teacher. During our stay in Abbi, my parents travelled around a lot, organising and arranging church meetings as usual, always leaving us in the care of adult female relatives or helpers.

During one of these trips, we were left with an older non-resident female helper. Alice was to look after us while my parents were away. When my parents did not return by 10pm that night, as arranged, the girl settled me, my younger brother and a younger male cousin, Daniel, for the night and left. My younger brother, my little male cousin and I (aged eight, nine and ten respectively) quickly fell fast asleep. My parents did not come home until the early hours of the following morning, around 2pm, because the lorry they were travelling in broke down in the middle of nowhere. We did not hear their return, nor their shouts and banging, so the door was not opened. We were very fast asleep and did not hear a sound! After a lot of wailing and commotion, my parents broke down the front door. We all woke up screaming! My parents thought we were dead, and we thought armed robbers had invaded the house! Many such risks, to their lives and their children's were sometimes taken in the process of their service to God and humanity, but their faith held firm.

One terrible day during lesson in Abbi primary school, one of our classroom mud walls suddenly collapsed on top of us as we sat listening to our teacher. Half the children in the class were buried under the rubble including myself. One ten year old girl, Mata, lost her life. Twenty-three children were injured and my left ankle was broken. The walls came down so suddenly that no one had time to escape. All the injured children were taken to the overflowing local dispensary from where my parents came to fetch me after treatment. To their great credit, my parents always took these difficult events in their stride. As my ankle healed slowly, I returned to school which was a mile away, taken every day on my father's bicycle by the young church gardener. The eighteen year old church gardener, Ocho, was a tall, dark-compexioned, kind, decent good-natured orphan boy who spent a lot of time with my family. He was like a son to my parents and a big brother to me and my brothers. He would sometimes take my younger brother fishing. In these Delta Riverine regions, we taught ourselves to swim in the very dangerous rapid-flowing Ethiope River (which ran and still runs through Abraka, Obiarukwu and Abbi), despite parental warning against this practice. We often swore each other to secrecy about our adventures but if we fell out, one of us would tell on the others. We loved making necklaces and earrings from seaweed plants. We also learned to catch small fish that often swam to the shallow end of the river with our bare hands, fetch fire wood, and cook various local dishes. By the age of eight, I could cook a decent meal for the whole family!

The height of my parents' professional life came when they were transferred to a city called Benin City in what was then Western Nigeria. Benin City, now the capital of Edo State of Nigeria, is a place renowned for the toughness of its people, their war-like disposition and their human sacrifices in ancient times. Benin City has strong traditions dating back to the fifteenth century when their contact with Europeans was established. In Benin City, the prominent ruler was and still is the Oba of Benin who is assisted by his chiefs. The Oba wears traditional costume made throughout of coral beads and his chiefs wear white flowing robes or are swathed in white and garlanded with coral beads. Oba's wives (they were and still are usually many) wear huge rapas round their bosoms. Their hair is made up in beehive fashion and adorned throughout with coral beads. The power of the Oba was supreme in the olden days. Two young boys carrying swords always stood (and still do) on each side of the Oba. My maternal grandmother was very distressed about this particular deployment to Benin City. She felt her only daughter had been sent into harm's way. But not my mother! She felt she had been catapulted into a wonderful new world of chances, and adventure. Benin City was a sprawling city with diverse opportunities for different ventures. My mother sensed wonderful opportunities, and so it turned out to be, because moving to Benin was a major turning point in her life and in all of our lives. For her, it was like a "renaissance," a rebirth and a new beginning. In fact, in Benin City, we found a lot of friendship, love and great achievements.

My mother threw herself into many businesses (such as household commodities and scrap metal) that came along and her businesses flourished. She met and struck up an enduring friendship with two other businesswomen in Benin, Mrs Agatha Ehiemua and Mrs Anne Okpaise. My mother and her two friends established an enterprise called ABAS Company, ABAS being their initials: Anne for Mrs Okpaise, Bernice for my mother and Agatha for Mrs Ehiemua. They were known as "the beautiful friends" and they were indeed beautiful. These three strong women (of same generation) were determined to make the world a better place. Very sadly, soon after the business was set up, Anne died suddenly of an asthma attack, but the two surviving friends carried on regardless until politics beckoned for my mother. Mrs Ehiemua, like my mother, was also deeply involved in political activism, and was a general contractor for a number of businesses. She was for many years the leader of the Ishan Women's Society in Bendel State and subsequently in Edo State which was carved out of Bendel State. My mother and Mrs Ehimua's strong friendship endured for the rest of their lives. Mrs Ehiemua had two sons and no daughter so she always called me her daughter and I looked upon her as a second mother. She passed away four months after my mother, aged eighty eight.

All kinds of businesses beckoned and became aspects of my mother's adventure. She was a general contractor for many businesses, namely, excavation of pipelines, building of schools, supplying sand and gravel, sale of foodstuff and building materials like cement, tar drums. She got contracts for bush clearing, digging of gutters, purchasing and selling of pipes for road building, house decorating and building modern houses. My mother was also a timber merchant supplying timber to AT&P (Africa Timber & Plywood Company) Sapele in the Niger Delta. Her major line was scrap-metal. She was an Associate of Buck Nigerian Ltd in Lagos, providing them with scrap metal which was shipped abroad. This company was set up by Mr Buck, a British businessman who was a very successful scrap metal dealer in Lagos in the 1950s and 1960s. My mother had strong young men who worked for her. She would travel by canoe in those dangerous times to carry merchandise for sale to

Baro in Northern Nigeria and Fernando Poo, now Bioko, part of Equatorial Guinea. In between she was buying and selling "Accra", cotton materials for making Nigerian traditional attire. She also occasionally travelled to Ghana, which was known as the Gold Coast at that time, to purchase gold jewellery for sale. Hence, what my father couldn't afford for my family, my mum was able to provide.

Business contracts were often distributed by the State and my mother was one of the contractors given the responsibility by the Bendel State government after the Biafran War in the 1970s to plant grass on the kerb-side of the motorway which ran from Benin City to Asaba. Though mainly a scrap metal dealer, my mother undertook many other business ventures. Her energy and zest for life was limitless. My brother George was at St. Augustine's Grammar School in Nkwerre in Eastern Nigeria. My mother took on the job of supplying foodstuffs to the school to supplement my brother's school fees when money was short. The principal of the school, Mr Ezekwesili, was so impressed by my mother's efforts that he asked her to be the godmother to his only son, Nnamdi. This was a great honour which my mother cherished all her life.

When work was plentiful, my mother wouldn't come home for days, sleeping in makeshift shacks in remote villages like, Sakpoba, Omelege and Nikorowa and other outbacks with her workers, breaking or dismantling iron or sawing wood awaiting shipment to Buck Nigerian Ltd and other business companies in Lagos. She was born for the outdoors and didn't mind travelling, though it couldn't have been easy, riding in rickety lorries' or trucks in the days of dust-roads, potholes and incompetent reckless drivers. She did all this, in order to give her children a decent education. Most of the time she hired the drivers she knew and would sit in the front seat beside them. The journeys were often hazardous and challenging. I missed my mother a lot during these absences, and I vowed to be a full-time housewife and mother, a situation which unfortunately never materialised. These absences were also difficult for the entire family, especially for my father as a clergyman, particularly when my mother missed prayer meetings (which were the responsibility of clergymen's wives to attend) or an important church occasion. However, the financial returns from my mother's business ventures often pacified my dad because she was making a very important contribution to the family. On one occasion, when my father was extremely concerned that my mother was going to miss the Good Friday service, he sent the gardener with an urgent letter for my mother to the very remote village where she was gathering scrap metal, asking her to return immediately with the driver. And she did return immediately with the driver!

In no time, my mother's first two lorries and a tipper were delivered to our Vicarage in Benin City. The top fronts of these vehicles were emblazoned (as the top-fronts of many Nigerian lorries were and still are) with the three words, "The Faithful Servant" meaning "we are faithful servants of the Lord". This slogan was a statement of my parents' belief that, "If you have faith, even as little as a mustard seed, you can say to this mountain, "move from here to there and it will move." (Matthew 17:20). Florence Scovel-Shinn (1925) states that "It is Faith that holds a vision steady and in due season we shall reap, if we faint not." (p.46) *The Game of Life and How to Play It)*

Some church members were baffled. The question on many lips was "how can a vicar's wife acquire all this when the Bible says our reward is in heaven and not on earth?" However, most people, including the fatherly Bishop Agori Iwe admired my mother's drive and courage. My father was always extremely proud of his wife! He always quoted 1 John 4:18,

"There is no fear in love ... Perfect love casts out fear."

5: THE ENTERPRISE YEARS

❋ ❋ ❋

"Do not go where the path may lead, go instead where there is no path and leave a trail."
Ralph Waldo Emerson (1803 – 1882)

Benin City was in Western Nigeria until the first republic was established in 1963. Mid-West State was created out of Western Nigeria. Mid-West State later became Bendel State in 1976. Bendel State was then partitioned in 1991 into Edo State and Delta State. Benin City is now the capital of Edo state and Asaba the capital of Delta State which is my family's home State.

The Kerry children loved Benin and learnt to speak the Edo language. From there we all went to our various secondary schools. George and I subsequently travelled to the United Kingdom in the early 1960s for further studies and was a feat for most Nigerian parents at that time. My parents had dreams about themselves and their children, dreams of success and a better future.

My mother's scrap metal depot in Benin was known as the "Stacking Yard" and was located in Igbesanwa Street, three miles from our St Paul's Vicarage. This was a fenced yard, a quarter of a mile square with some shacks for storing metal and various merchandise. My mother always had green fingers, so planted two mango fruits trees and an orange tree in this yard which thrived and were regularly weighed down by loads of popular sweet succulent fruits loved and shared by many. My mother's green fingers extended beyond her stacking yard. Our family home in Owerre-Olubor, on a large piece of land, half a mile square, was surrounded by orchards of oranges, avocados, mangoes, guava, lime trees, lemon trees, grape-fruits and numerous edible herbs and vegetables. Coconut, banana and plantain trees were everywhere and so were the odd pineapples. Fruits and vegetables grew easily and wildly in Nigeria but when nurtured did even better. This large ten bed-room family home (along old Umunede/Ogwashi-Ukwu Road) was built single-handedly by my mother and furnished with old furniture purchased from her white business partners returning to the UK.

Apart from Mr Buck (of Buck Nigeria Ltd) my mother's other business partners were Mr and Mrs Drew (who worked at the saw mill in Sapele) and Mr Gam in Lagos. She worked very successfully with these partners and they had great respect for her. Mr Buck would sometimes visit our home in Benin City but always sat in the verandah. He never came into the house and always refused the offer of any food or drink. He also took many photos of us during his visits although we never saw these photos. However, I remember him showing my parents a home movie he made of me walking from our front gate to our front door. I was in my mid-teens and wearing my mother's hand-made green floral dress with small sleeves. We were thrilled, but that was it! We weren't given any copy of these photographs and as far I know my parents never asked and didn't seem to mind anyway. Mrs Drew once gave my mother a lovely present of two beautiful chunky hand-knitted sweaters, one red and one white. My mother liked and spoke well of Mrs Drew, whom I never met, but I remember Mr Buck as a cheerful large man. In fact, he was larger than life. He had, what I now realise, a slight German accent. I knew he had a wife and three children based in Putney in London. He didn't live long though because by the time I visited his family in London in 1962, he had passed away, his wife informed me.

Usually, when the many white expatriates finished their stint in our part of Nigeria, they would sell the entire contents of their houses. These included nearly-new furniture and household equipment: chairs, iron beds, glass windows, baths, sinks, kitchen utensils like food blenders - everything. My mother often bought the items she could afford, and re-used or re-sold them. Much of the rescued furniture, as already stated, were utilised to furnish and adorn our family country home in Owerre-Olubor.

During the pinnacle of my mother's business enterprises, the sound of our big lorries arriving at dawn or in the evenings signalling my mother's imminent return, would send us all rushing into the front yard to check the lorries' cargo. They were often loaded with scrap metal, planks of wood and foodstuffs, and returned, up to a day or two before my mother. On one particular day, one of our "Faithful Servants" was loaded with glass windows (4ft by3ft) with their hinges still attached. Everyone in the house, except my dad usually helped to offload whatever cargo arrived. I was fourteen or fifteen years old and on holidays from secondary school. We carried two average-sized windows at a time on our heads into the front store room. Suddenly the glass of my windows gave way and collapsed around my neck and stuck there like a square jagged glass necklace with its frame still intact. I didn't realise the glass was cracked. I was screaming in pain and fear with my neck lacerated and bleeding. My father rushed to my rescue and smashed the rest of the glass to release my head. Luckily, I was not seriously hurt. That was a frightening experience, but the incident did not deter me from future involvement in my mother's work whenever I could. We were all always involved in our own various ways

Occasionally, oblong gas cylinders, about six feet long and three feet in diameter were delivered to our vicarage. I am not sure how they were used, but it was used in cutting up metal in the Stacking Yard before shipment. On one particular day, about twelve gas cylinders were delivered to await my mother's return. The following morning very early, we experienced an alarming rude awakening by an earth-shattering blast like one long sound of a giant horn. We all rushed out at once, to discover that, probably due to pressure from within the cylinder, or a loose screw, one cylinder had blasted itself open. This deafening blast went on for about six minutes – though it seemed like eternity - until all the gas escaped. No one knew what to do so we all just stood there watching helplessly. My father was very concerned about us but didn't really know what to do. Was the cylinder going to explode next? No one knew. We could see the force of the air coming out from the nozzle of the cylinder. Suddenly, it blew itself out and stopped, leaving a huge crater of about six feet in circumference on the ground. For years we laughed about this but it was certainly nightmarish at the time.

Many people marvelled at my mother's hard work, grit and determination. Despite her slender frame, she was nicknamed "igwe" (iron) because she was strong and rarely ill.

My mother possessed incredible confidence and vivacity. Everyone who met her wanted to speak to her because she had intellectual appeal and sexual magnetism and radiated youthful exuberance. The Bishop's sermon at her funeral in 2005 summed up and celebrated all these qualities. He said, "Mrs

Kerry was unlike any other woman I know. She worked hard and achieved so much through her own strength. She believed in herself and what she could do for others."

An eminent chief in my State (Chief Ofulue) once said to my mother:

"Mrs Kerry, you know what? I have known you for a long time and have come to the conclusion that you appear so great, so decent and so sanctified that no one can harm you. Anyone hating you or spitting at you is like spitting at the heavens because the spittle rains back down on their heads".

My mother was always impeccably dressed and looked regal. I could confidently say that she was a fashion icon in her time. She believed, like Polonius in Shakespeare's "Hamlet", that "The apparel oft proclaims the man." For this unsurpassed elegance, I always aspired to look like my mother. She was chic and feminine: slim and effortlessly beautiful inside and outside. When she swept into a room, she lit it up. She glowed and looked incredible in whatever she wore and was outstanding in every sense of the word. With the ability to look fantastic at all times, she made the best of everything she had. She was my hero and role model, delightful and fascinating to the end. Age could not detract from her beauty.

My mother cherished the gifts God gave her but was never affected by them. She was never proud or arrogant. In fact she possessed a great deal of humility. She appreciated every kindness shown to her by others. She had profound wisdom, extraordinary insight, faultless judgement and intuition. Empathising with people was one of her great assets and her life was generally joyous. My mother taught me to always look impeccable and to smile always. "First impressions last forever my daughter," she would say. Her mouth sparkled with a complete set of pearly beautiful teeth all her life. I can never match my mother's standards, but she'll always be my inspiration.

These words of the American president, George Washington (1732–1799), describing his mother, capture how I felt and still feel about my mother:

"My mother was the most beautiful woman I ever saw. All I am I owe to my mother. I attribute all my success in life to the moral, intellectual and physical education I received from her."

My mother was my education and I owe it all to her!

Mothering Sundays at St. Paul's Ibo Church, Benin City, were outstanding and memorable occasions. The Mothers' Union and Women's Guild were often galvanised by my mother for these special Sundays. My mother compiled all the songs (known as "native airs") in the Mothering Sunday Hymn book, which was regularly used on Mothering Sundays. People from surrounding churches came to watch and participate.

**Beautiful friends 1960. Left to right: Mrs Anne Okpaise,
Mrs Bernice Kerry and Mrs Agatha Ehiemua**

Harvest Festivals were even more amazing. A member of the congregation once said that it was so heart-warming to watch Mrs Kerry leading the ladies, in all their glory, up the church aisle for harvest thanks-giving. My mother would sashay to and from the church aisle to the altar, with the women dancing behind her to the sound of hymn singing and Ibo choruses with the sound of drums and piano accompaniment. Mrs Kerry "waves inside her clothes," one Bishop complimented her during the Mothers' Union Centenary Conference which she attended in London in 1976. The best meals were cooked and served at harvest festivals, all supervised by my mother. Our Bishop loved the work which my parents were doing, the congregation were happy participants and my father was proud of his church and his wife. St Paul's Ibo Church was always teeming with believers, all from Benin City and the surrounding villages.

Nigerians are colourful dressers, especially their women. People dress as elegantly or as simply as they can afford, but are always colourful. Our traditional clothes are often interspersed with western clothes especially among the young and professionals. The commonest style is "up and down", made up of a top which can have sleeves or be sleeveless and two "rapas or wrappers"(usually cotton patterned materials), one of 2 ½ yards, tied round the waist to reach the ankle and the other of 2 yards)tied round the midriff to reach the knees. They are sewn in a special way to achieve these effects. The younger generation today add more style to their "rapas," sewing them into long fashionable skirts and wearing them with an appropriate top. A single yard of the same material is tied round the head in whatever flamboyant style people prefer. On the other hand, white lace tops are worn with "abada", "jorje", "damask", "Ankara" or "silk" rapas – all different materials for making Nigerian attire. Nigerian women love wearing head-pieces, especially the stiff head-gear known as "haze" or gele. This takes mastery to tie; fold in two in the form of a triangle, place round the head from the back, flick one end to the right, the other to the left, and then tie or tuck round the head at the back where it sits like a huge hat, which can be stored for re-use. My mother was a master head-gear fixer and I still haven't got a clue how it's done! My mother usually did it for me or would do it on her own head, and gently lift it onto my head.

The Yorubas of Western Nigeria often wear "iro" and "buba". The "buba" is a big blouse with huge sleeves. The "rapa" or "iro" is tied round the midriff on top of the blouse to reach the knee or calf. Another yard of the same material is draped over the shoulder. This outfit is topped with a huge one yard piece of head gear. Nigerian women love all manner of jewellery (coral beads, gold, silver, costume jewellery) and are often draped in or dripping with them. Nigerian men are equally vibrant, with their loose colourful clothes of trousers ("shokoto") and loose shirt-like tops reaching the knee or longer, depending on preference. On special occasions an "agbada" is worn on top of this long shirt. An "agbada" is a v-necked, wide-armed piece of clothing sewn to reach the ground. Men usually top this outfit with a small cap called a "fila." The outfit could be complemented, on special occasions, with gold or coral beads round the neck and wrists.

My mother had an extraordinary capacity for friendship and a heart of gold. She had a brilliant mind and so was always such good company that people gave her their attention. She loved beautiful things and beautiful people and she lived her life as if her mission was, to have been sent into the world for a particular purpose: to help and inspire others, as I believe it was. People sent for Mrs Kerry if they were sick or in hardship and she rarely failed them. Throughout her whole life, she was loving, cherishing and fiercely and staunchly loyal. If you told my mother you were a dustman or road sweeper, she would say "well done my child" and would proceed to tell the world how proud she was of what you do and how important it was for the entire world. She was most encouraging in every way.

One of my mother's inspirational pieces, which she often read to me was sent to her on a post card by Dr Nnamdi

Azikiwe, with a photo of himself and his wife, Flora. It was this inspirational poem by Douglas Mallock (1877 – 1938):

Be the Best of Whatever You Are

"If you can't be a pine on the top of a hill;
Be a scrub in the valley - but be
The best little scrub by the side of the hill;
Be a bush if you can't be a tree.

If you can't be a bush, be a bit of the grass,
And some highway some happier make:
If you can't be a Muskie then just be a bass -
But the liveliest bass in the lake!

We can't all be Captains', we've got to be crew,
There's something for all of us here.
There's big work to do and there's lesser to do,
And the task we must do is near.

If you can't be a highway then just be a trail,
If you can't be the sun, be a star;
It isn't by size that you win or you fail
Be the best of whatever you do!"

Best of all, I never knew my mother to hold a grudge because she was always fearless and straight with people. She said what she had to say, and did what she had to do, and that was that!

I never lacked confidence because my mother always built up my self-esteem. Every day, she told me I was beautiful and the best and called me beautiful pet names, like Titi (baby, girl), Ada (first daughter), Egy (coined from grace, etc . She was the best friend that any child could have. In fact, my mum and I were "joined at the hip" all our lives and she was always there for me and her eyes and thoughts were always on me, like a tigress, looking out for danger and protecting her cubs.

In the 1950s in Nigeria, schoolchildren in Standard 5 and 6 (equivalent to years 5 and 6 in UK primary schools) took what were known as entrance examinations to get into various secondary schools in the country. In 1952, I passed three entrance examinations, gaining places at three of the best girls secondary schools in Nigeria, namely, Queen's College, Ede, in the Western state of Nigeria, St Anne's College, Ibadan, also in the West and Archdeacon Crowther Memorial Girls' School (ACMGS) Elelenwa, near Port Harcourt in Eastern Nigeria. The centre for these examinations for us was CMS Girls' Primary School in Benin City where I was a pupil, but the interviews were held at the respective secondary schools. After careful deliberation on my successes, my parents decided to send me to Archdeacon Crowther Memorial Girls' School in the East. The main reason I can think of for this decision is because they were both educated in Eastern Nigeria (Awka and St Monica's Ugwu-ogba) and for many years carried out their church ministry there and made many friends along the way.

Going for the final selection for admission, I was accompanied by my mother who always planned everything in advance. Travelling to Port Harcourt for this interview, we left from Benin by road in the government-owned Armel's Transport (lorry) to Asaba. These lorries had wooden seats at the back and two extra seats in front, next to the driver's. My mum usually arranged for us to sit in the front seats. It was somehow safer. This was a two hour drive of seventy-seven miles over rough terrain of potholes and poorly tarred roads. From Asaba, we crossed to Onitsha by the official licensed ferry (the Shanahan) over the three miles length of the River Niger. The Shanahan took thirty minutes to make this trip and the unlicensed, less safe open boats took forty-five minutes to cross the river. However, people sometimes risked the canoes if they missed the Shanahan.

Thankfully, a modern bridge now connects Asaba to Onitsha over River Niger. From Onitsha we boarded another lorry going to PortHarcourt, ninety-eight miles away.

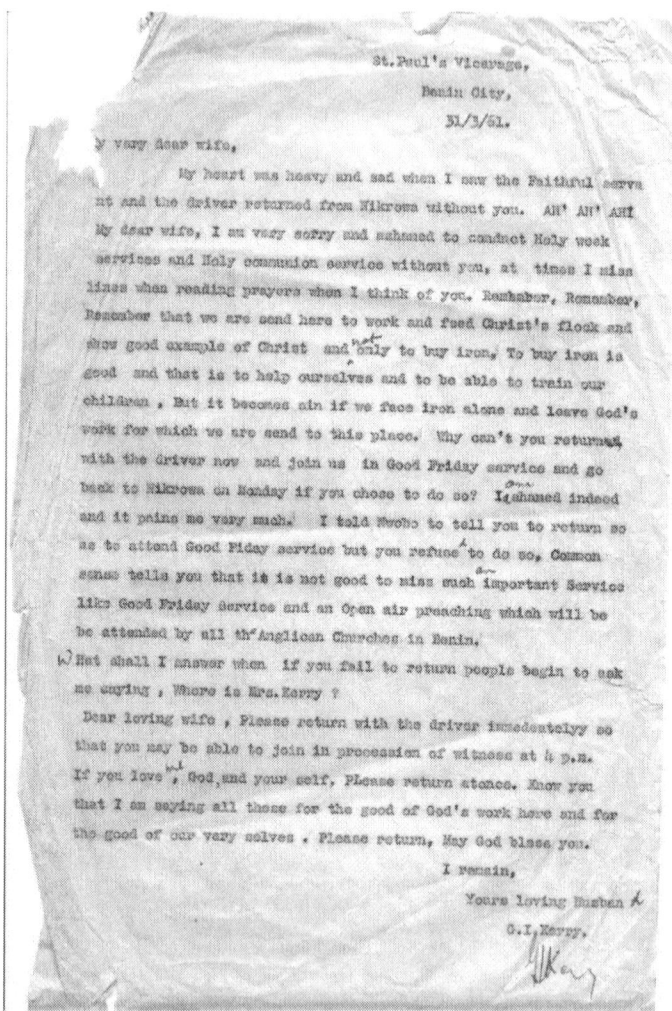

Letter from my father to my mother to return home

From there we took another lorry to Elelenwa village, a distance of eight miles, to the quiet isolated area where the school was situated. The roads were rough and dusty through towns and villages. My mother was always an early riser and would wake me at about 5am for any adventure together. We slept at a family friend's in Port Harcourt. We woke early the following day, had a bucket bath, got dressed, and then off we went to board a lorry travelling to ACMGS, Elelenwa.

Days before, my mother would also have worked out what friends or relatives we would be spending the night with at Asaba or Onitsha or Port Harcourt, on the way to the interview venue which was Archdeacon Crowther Memorial Girl' School, Elelenwa. Any of these places was a possible stopover to spend the night before continuing to our destination. This pattern of travel was to be repeated for the six years I spent in the secondary school. The night before my interview, we slept at our family friends home, the Ofors in PortHarcourt and on the morning of the interview for selection, we were up early, bathed, dressed and had the offered breakfast. Often, we were in a rush to move on and would buy food for a quick bite to eat by the roadside, like roast yam or plantain, or go into a road-side cafe to buy some cooked food.

My parents were very proud of me passing three 'entrance examinations' and so were all the parents of children who were clever enough and lucky enough to pass their secondary school entrance examinations. It was a source of joy and pride to their parents if and when their children passed these exams but it was a source of envy too for parents whose children failed their entrance examinations. I remember one church elder saying sarcastically to my parents when told I had passed this entrance examination, "You're already struggling with George's school fees, how are you going to cope with this additional burden?" But my mother always liked a challenge and was a great believer in the adage that" he who laughs last, laughs best."

On the day of the interview, I dressed in my Sunday best, a floral pink dress with tiny flowers, with a small white collar and short sleeves, which my mother's friend Mrs Nicolls made for me. I wore a new brown pair of sandals that my father had bought from Leanards shoe shop in Benin, specifically for this occasion. I'm not sure who was more excited - my mother or me! It was a lovely day in May, sunny and hot. May is my birth month and it always brings me luck.

We were met at the school gate at 8am by two teachers, a white teacher, Miss Backhouse and Miss Obi, a young Nigerian teacher. Miss Backhouse was frenetic, spoke fast and had a quick walk. Miss Obi on the other hand was quiet, a bit shy and relaxed. The school was on a fairly huge piece of land, lush with vegetation and dotted with unsophisticated colonial-style buildings mainly bungalows and dormitories, with a small basic mud-built chapel roofed with corrugated iron sheets. Huge flamboyant trees (*delonix regia*) were dotted here and there around the sprawling compound and bougainvillea, hibiscus plants and frangipani shrubs were everywhere. It was a CMS missionary school, and half the teaching staff were white and half, were ethnic Nigerians. We were all in all, one hundred young girls, ushered into a large room. The room had normal school desks and chairs. We sat and awaited the grand entrance of the principal, Miss Marjorie Hill who was English. Our parents and guardians were advised to look round the school and Elelenwa village if they wished and to return at about 2pm. When Miss Hill entered, we all stood up as advised by Miss Backhouse and she welcomed us with a little lecture on good behaviour. Miss Hill, unlike tall wiry Miss Backhouse, was a petite middle-aged woman, plain but attractive in a kind of way. She appeared strict, spoke firmly and did not smile much. In 2003, I read, by chance, her obituary in a British newspaper. She lived to be one hundred and one years old, with an MBE. After Miss Hill's welcome and address, we were given a written test, in English Arithmetic and General Knowledge, under the supervision of Miss Backhouse and Miss Obi. This took an hour and half. Then we were called, one by one, into the school library for the oral interview, administered by two other white teachers, Miss Wall and Miss Jolly. Miss Wall looked angry, with a tall, stiff wooden gait and walk and not very friendly. She hardly ever smiled unlike Miss Jolly who was exactly as her name suggested, short, plump and cheerful. She was an excellent English teacher and we all loved her. As you entered the room for the oral interview, you were inspected. You were asked to turn round and round again. "How old are you? Was your dress tidy? Hair cut short and combed? (No plaits or straightened hair was allowed). Smiled enough? Looked Miss Hill, Miss Wall and Miss Jolly in the eye while answering their questions? What's your name? What's your date of birth? What's your surname? What's your father's occupation? Where have you travelled from? Then followed the general knowledge test: "What disease do tsetse flies cause? What disease do mosquitoes carry? Who were Mongo Park and David Livingstone? When did the gospel come to the Niger? Why is Lagos a colony? Who is Archdeacon Crowther?" And so on and so forth. The oral interview took about thirty to forty-five minutes per student. Most of the answers I knew, so I felt good afterwards. The school would be sending the result to our parents. I met a girl called Rose at that interview. Both of us were offered places, were in the same year and still firmly in touch.

My mother was so thrilled to see me when she got back to collect me. "Egi (her pet name for me) how did it go? Were they nice to you? Were the questions hard or easy? I hope you are not starving?" she asked excitedly, all the questions almost tumbling out at once. She gave me a huge hug when I said everything went well, except that sometimes I had to listen carefully to understand what the white teachers were saying because they spoke so fast. "You will learn, my daughter", she said.

After the interview, we made our way back to Port Harcourt by lorry where we slept overnight, again, with the Ofors, thanked them in the morning for their hospitality, bid them farewell and left. We hurried to the motor garage to catch a lorry heading in our direction towards Onitsha. Where-ever we spent the night, my mother made sure she took some kind of foodstuff as a thank you present for our hosts. These are usually some smoked fish, yams or "garri" (dried grated cassava root) or both.

My father's ordination as a priest in 1954 was a very joyful occasion for the family, so my mother was well prepared for it. She bought two beautiful dresses for both of us and bought two hats to match our individual dresses. The special day arrived, and we were all dressed to kill. Then, I started making a fuss. I preferred my mother's hat to mine! "How can you have my hat when the hats were made to match our individual dresses?" my mother asked impatiently. "I just like your hat more than mine," I persisted. All her persuasive skills to make me see sense failed, and we were running late. Eventually, my mother gave up and swapped her hat for my small hat. How many mothers would do that? There were many episodes like that throughout our lives. I was sometimes very wilful and would say "no" instead of "yes" and vice vrsa.

I lost a baby in 1980 in Benin City and my mother camped beside me in hospital, day and night, for the two days it took. She never abandoned her children at any stage of our lives, but gave such great love and care that many of our contemporaries were envious. She frequently brought us presents, like food stuff, especially, yam, garri, plantain, smoked fish and even expensive fabrics to make Nigerian clothes.

Soon after I had first arrived in the UK, I met a Nigerian girl of my own age called Chi-chi who had known my family well. She told me that she often wished my mother was her mother. Her words showed how my mother touched people's lives. What she said really meant a lot to me. I've met many people who admired my mother and had nothing but praise for her human touch, and effort.

During my brief return to Nigeria in the 1970s, I met a man called Mr Ehi at a teachers/parents' meeting. His daughter Olive was in the same class in secondary school as my daughter Nicky. We struck up a conversation about Nigerian women, and suddenly he said that he had known an exceptional Nigerian woman when he was the work supervisor at AT&P, Sapele. This woman was different from the normal Nigerian women he knew. "This madam", he said, "would come to the Saw-mill with her workers and stayed with them the whole day, dismantling and sorting iron, without eating or taking a break while they worked". He proceeded to describe this "hardworking" lady, saying she was tall, dark and beautiful and that she was a vicar's wife in Benin City. I felt really proud and Mr Ehi couldn't believe it when I told him that woman was my mother! "Oh," he laughed, "I can see some resemblance. Fancy, it's a small world!" he exclaimed. When I told my mother about my discussion with Mr Ehi, she remembered the man, whom she said would kindly bring her sandwiches on occasions, encouraging her to take a break.

I visited my best friend Aggy in Kaduna, Northern Nigeria, in 1978 when I lived in Benin City, Bendel State. When I was returning to Benin, she gave me a parcel for her mother who lived in Ishan, about a hundred miles from Benin. Though I took the parcel, I didn't know how or when I was going to deliver it because of my work and the distance. As soon as I mentioned this to my mother, she quickly offered to deliver the parcel to my friend's mother by herself. "Aggy is my daughter too", my mother said, and even though the family car was not available at that time, my mother hired a taxi to travel all that way, over sixty miles from Agbor where she lived, to deliver the parcel. This was my mother: a faithful friend and a friend of my friends! My friend's family often remembered this deed and it bound our two families closer together. My friend Aggy, looked out for my mother and showered her with a lot of kindness when I returned to the UK.

The constant support all the family received from my mother was legendary and well-documented, whether it involved taking us to entrance exams, visiting us regularly in boarding schools, paying fees, purchasing clothes and food or buying presents for our teachers. She did it all with pride and joy. My father was always there to support her.

Teachers were often very impressed with my mother due to her care of her children. She replaced all our school gear and equipment without anger or rebuke when they were carelessly lost or stolen, and replaced money that had been thoughtlessly spent. She made sure we lacked nothing in school, so much so, that my brother George was nicknamed "money na san san" meaning, "money is in abundance like sand".

My elder brother George, who looked physically like my mother, also inherited her competitiveness and sporting prowess. He won many trophies for sports: the pole vault, high jump and sprinting. Though only 5ft 10ins, he was an all-round sports-man, and his athletic achievements continued during his studies overseas. He won many sporting trophies in India during his medical studies. He was ambitious too and always wanted to be a medical doctor. So when he finished his secondary school education, my parents (my mother in particular) decided he should go to the UK for further studies. Such was my parents' ambition for their children, because during the 1950s and the 1960s, it was financially impossible for most Nigerian families to afford educating their children in good secondary schools in Nigeria, let alone abroad.

Initially, George went to Lampeter University in Wales to study theology, as my father had hoped, but left because he really wanted to study medicine. He needed the relevant subjects to do that, so he enrolled in Paddington Technical College in London, where he met the late great musician Fela Onikolakpo Kuti. They became house-mates and great friends. My brother said that even then, Fela showed great flair for music and singing and was always jolly. The friendship lasted until Fela passed away in 1998. The two friends also had something else in common. Fela's mother, Mrs Fumilayo Ransome-Kuti (1900 – 1978) was, in her time, a political activist and the Yoruba women's leader in Western Nigeria just as my mother was also involved in Nigerian politics. From Paddington Technical College, my brother proceeded to Heidelberg University in Vienna, where again things didn't work out as planned. Fortunately for our family, my mother was appointed a Senate Member of Parliament in the first Nigerian Republic (1963-1966) around the same time that India was offering scholarships to Nigerians interested in studying medicine in India. My mother took the opportunity, supported by the Senate speaker Chief Dr Nwafor Orizu, (alias "akwa-eke" due to his good looks), to secure a scholarship for her son to study medicine in Bombay, India. Thus my brother left for India in 1966 and qualified as a medical doctor in 1971 after which he returned to Nigeria in 1972.

Meanwhile, when my younger brother Patrick finished his secondary school education at Ubulu-Ukwu Grammar School, in Bendel State, my parents made sure his life did not lack purpose. He was tall, (6ft) good looking, articulate and charismatic and still is. Though he excelled in sports, especially football, he was encouraged to do more A-Levels in order to go to university. This he eventually did, finishing successfully with a degree in Education in 1979 followed by his National Youth Service programme, which all Nigeria University graduates carried out and still carry out for character-building and to serve their country. He was sent to the Youth camp at Ogwu, near Enugu in Enugu State. The most remarkable thing about my mother at this time was that she insisted on going with her son to see for herself where he was going to serve out his youth service. She did all of this even though this camp was up a steep hill which she climbed easily at the age of sixty-six!

After my father passed away in July 1981, my mother encouraged Patrick to go back to university to study law which had always been his ambition. His legal studies were completely financed by my mother who also took on the upbringing of his three young sons, Ekene, aged six, Chukwuka (Achu) aged five and Onyi aged two, after his marriage broke down. My mother loved the experience of looking after her grandchildren because she experienced joy in nurturing people. Her love for all her grandchildren was all-encompassing and she interacted regularly with most of them.

Sometimes my parents borrowed money when things were hard, especially to pay our school fees and there were two occasions which remain vivid in my memory. The first was when my parents borrowed money for my school fees from Mr and Mrs Itoha, a fairly wealthy couple in Benin City. Burke Nigerian Ltd in Lagos was late in payment for goods delivered to the company and I had to return to school. I can't remember how much money it was that was borrowed but my parents couldn't repay the money when they said they would. It was during one of our holidays that this couple decided their debt must be paid. They came every morning, early, threatening brimstone and fire. They came every day, for a week, screaming my parents name at the top of their voices so the neighbours could hear what was going on at the vicarage. It was a very embarrassing situation for my parents.

On this particular day, knowing the couple were coming and there was no money to give them, my parents went to pray in the church vestry - they always did this when times were hard because we always lived near or in the church compound. My parents usually went around 5 a.m to pray and were in the vestry praying when the couple arrived at our house at 6am in the morning, yelling for their money. Mrs Itoha shouted the loudest, both in pidgin English and in Benin language. When the couple were told that my parents were in the church praying, they stormed over there, shouting as loud as they could, but my parents stayed put. They just knelt there praying. We were all cowering in the house wondering what the Itohas were going to do next, because they were quite wealthy and well- known in Benin. I was really upset for my parents because my family had known Itohan family for many years and we thought they were true friends. After about two hours, the couple left. This was a couple who lacked nothing in terms of what most Nigerians had at that time and could have waited a little longer for their money! I believe the debt was paid eventually, though I never knew how or when.

The second instance was when another businessman, Mr Oli, came down from Onitsha one early morning to ask for the money owed him through a business transaction with my mother. When he arrived, we told him my mother was away travelling, though she was still in bed. Angrily, he insisted that he would wait for her no matter how long it took. My father, who was often caught up in all this, couldn't persuade the man to return another day. My mother just stayed in her bedroom and didn't come out all day but the man stayed on, only leaving the house to buy food in the afternoon. The situation was becoming unbearable, so in the evening my father sent for a close family friend, Michael, who went and borrowed money from his friend to give to my parents to pay this businessman. Eventually, the businessman left without any "thank you" or "goodbye." In fact, he was quite angry when he left.

Many years later, in 1997, my brother Patrick and I encountered Mrs Itoha in Benin market. This was one half of the couple who went to scream at my parents in the church all those years ago. She greeted us very warmly and apologised profusely about how she and her husband behaved to my parents all those years ago, especially for not giving them enough time to finish praying, let alone time to pay up. We assured her my parents had forgiven and forgotten. I was really surprised that they did have a conscience after all!

My mother was an optimist and negative emotion was something she kept well under wraps except in very exceptional circumstances. She was stoical in the face of real hardship, and often stood by people in the most trying of times. She had great compassion and empathy towards people who were suffering and it was important for my mother to stand up for widows who frequently suffered great injustices in the Nigerian culture. In certain parts of Delta State, widows were often blamed for the death of their husbands and were subjected to horrific cruelty and brutality. Widows had their heads shaved and were made to wear black for at least a year. Sometimes kola nuts were placed on their husbands' coffins and these women were forced to pick them up with their mouths to prove they had nothing to do with their husband's demise. They were made to sleep on bare hard floors covered with local mats for weeks. My mother always categorically stated her objection to such cruel and unjustified practices and sometimes kept vigil with these widows for days and weeks and even insisted on sleeping on the floor with them. The kola nut is the nut of the kola tree, native to the tropical rainforest of West Africa. It is an important aspect of traditional culture and chewed by most Nigerians. It is used as a sacred offering during important life events, such as naming ceremonies, weddings and funerals.

6: THE SENATE YEARS: THE BEGINNING OF POLITICAL ACTIVISM

* * *

"Prove me now herewith, saith the Lord, if I
will not open you the windows of heaven, and
pour you out a blessing, that there shall not be
room enough to receive it."
Malachi 3: 1.

In March 1964, my mother was offered a political appointment as a Mid-Western Senator, to represent the women of the state in the Federal House of Senate in Lagos. She was the first Mid-West (later, Bendel State) lady senator and one of the two first Nigerian lady senators. She was nominated by merit and popular vote by the Mid-West government of the first Nigerian Republic, 1963-1966. Her other female contemporary at the Senate was Mrs Wuraola Esan, who represented the women in Western Nigeria in the Federal House of Senate in Lagos.

My mother's appointment came out of the blues and was a huge surprise to my family. She was away on a business trip as usual when an urgent letter arrived at the vicarage where my parents lived, from the Prime Minister at that time, Sir Dennis Osadebe. He wanted an immediate audience with my mother and also my father. My father couldn't fathom why the Prime Minister wanted to see them. They were not particularly involved in politics at that time, although my mother did campaign for Zik (Dr Nnamdi Azikiwe) of the NCNC (National Council of Nigeria and the Cameroon) in the early 1950s at my father's post in Abbi.

My parents with prime minister Sir Dennis Osadebay (left) and wife

Nevertheless, on receiving the Prime Minister's message, my father sent his driver to collect my mother from the remote Sakpoba village, near Sapele where she was dismantling scrap metal. When my parents arrived at the Government House which was the Prime Minister's residence, Sir Dennis congratulated my mother, breaking the incredible news. He informed her that a vote was carried in her favour by Mid-West women, when they were asked who they would like to represent them in the Federal House of Senate in Lagos.

Mum and Senator Wura Eson 1965

1967

All the women's groups nominated my mother, because over the years, they had observed, respected and appreciated her hard work and leadership qualities. At first, it was difficult for my parents to assimilate the incredible news. This appointment was going to change so many things!

Reverend Kerry with Bishop Agori Iwe 1967

Apart from my mother representing the State in the Senate and regularly travelling to Lagos whenever the House was in session, the post involved many other political commitments and meetings.

My father was justifiably very proud of his wife, but wondered what the Church would think. Happily and luckily, Bishop Agori Iwe, the Diocesan Bishop at that time sent my parents a hearty congratulatory message and constantly supported them thereafter.

1964 – Mrs Kerry with Senate members

Mrs Kerry with another Senator and Orderly 1964

Though my father had a Morris Minor car at this time, my mother was able to purchase a bigger family car: the first Citroen car owned by a woman in Benin City. People were fascinated by this car, because it crouched when not in motion but slowly rose when the engine was switched on, ready for take-off. Some people borrowed this car for their family weddings which gave my mother joy.

Our Bishop was a huge godly man who loved truth and humanity, all 6ft 8ins of him. He liked and appreciated my parents' work, because it positively promoted the work of the church as a whole.

1965 – Mrs Kerry standing behind the Prime
Minister, Sir Abubakar Tafawa Balewa

My mother's role in the Anglican community continued and in 1963 was awarded a Leadership Certificate for her services to the church. She was a member of the National Council of Women's Society (NCWS) and its President in the Ika Local Government Area from 1968 until 1995. In addition to this, she was a member of the Anglican Diocesan Synod of Benin City from 1962 until 1978, as well as being the regular organiser of women's prayer meetings, the Women's Guild and an active leader of the Anglican Mother's Union in the Benin Diocese.

In 1965, by virtue of her senatorial position, my mother was the designated Senate delegate to the Far East and was the only woman appointed by the federal government as part of the delegation for the opening of the Railway Extension in Maduiguri, Northern Nigeria. The organised trip to the Far East in 1965 was subsequently aborted due to the Indian / Pakistani conflict.

My mother played her Senate role to perfection. She regularly argued for women's rights, as she had done all her life. She defended the oppressed and fought for the defenceless. Her Senate years were definitely eventful and she loved the challenges that came with it. She was a fluent, articulate and charismatic speaker, both in English and Ibo. Her great strength was speaking up for women during parliamentary debates as recorded in the Hansard of the House of Senate. For example, in one parliamentary debate, which is recorded in the Senate Official report (Vol. 13, No.9, pp.32 & 381) dated Tuesday, 14th April 1964, my mother stated clearly what she thought about the insufficient funding allocated for work with women in society and gave her advice to all Nigerian women on how to care for their children.

Her contributions were still remembered many years later. Prince Nwafor Orizu, the Leader of the Senate at that time, acknowledged her political role in his 1993 publication: "The Leadership We Want - the contribution Mrs Kerry made to Nigerian politics." He made a clear reference to the role my mother played during her time in the House of Senate.

Archbishop Makarious the Third of Cyprus visited Nigeria in 1965. He asked my mother who was a senator at that time, "You are steeped in the church, how do you manage to mix politics with religion?" My mother's answer was immediate, simple and straight- forward, that is, that religion should be akin to politics. They both should genuinely love and serve humanity and strive for peace in the world.

Mrs Kerry with Mrs Wura Esan

However, my mother's Senate years were cut short by the sudden and disastrous military coup of January 1966. If my mother had stayed longer in the Senate, I am convinced many opportunities would have opened up for her to reach out and do more beyond the shores of Nigeria. However when the coup happened, she and her colleagues were marooned in Lagos because the Senate was in session at that time. There was a total news blackout throughout the country and my father and the rest of the family were frantic with worry. I was visiting Nigeria from the UK at that time and no one knew whether my mother was dead or alive.

It was worse for parliamentarians whose homes were far from Lagos in Western and Eastern Nigeria. They couldn't leave their hotels, let alone head for home to escape the problems caused by the coup. There were military road blocks everywhere. Undisciplined soldiers stopped and searched people every couple of miles, stealing and taking whatever they wanted from people with impunity. Rumours were rife of death and destruction, which eventually proved correct. The federal Prime Minister, Sir Abubakar Tafewa Balewa; the Premier of Northern Nigeria, the Saduana of Sokoto, Sir Ahmadu Bello; the Minister for Finance,

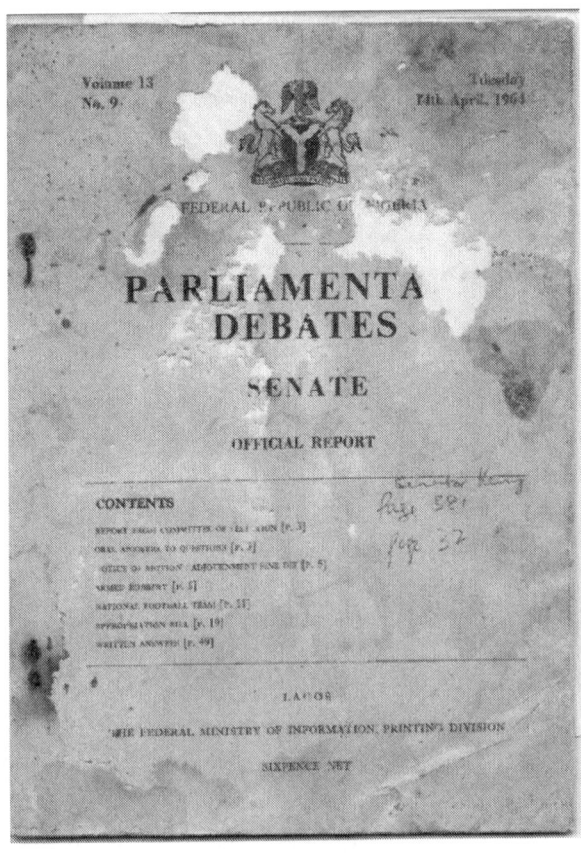

Chief Festus Okotie Eboh (alias "Omimi-Ejo") and the Premier of Western Nigeria, Sir Ladoke Akintola had been murdered.

The nation was unpredictable and in chaos! Everyone was deeply fearful about what further atrocities might occur.

Our family was very concerned about the possible outcome of all of the turmoil. They knew how horrific the outcome of wars can be. Then, my mother returned! Her driver drove the three hundred miles, through bush tracks to get them to Benin. She said, "I knew somehow I'd get home safely." She was an eternal optimist, always very confident and positive about her life, and indeed life in general. My mother's optimism was not unfounded, because after three days stranded in Lagos, she and her driver arrived safely back home hale and hearty. We couldn't wait to hear how they managed to get through all the army road checks, checkpoints and bush tracks. But my mother was a survivor!

That coup changed everything. People were euphoric about it but simultaneously fearful and stricken with dread at the thought of the unknown future. My parents were reluctant to leave Benin at this stage but were forced to flee to their rural homeland by the events that followed the outbreak of the Nigeria / Biafran war in 1967.

Before the Biafran war started, my parents carried on their church ministry in Benin City and my mum still continued with her various businesses as much as events would allow, making the best of a very difficult situation.

The murder of most of the senior politicians and some minor politicians caused outrage among some sections of society. Those leaders not murdered were incarcerated in prison.

The seismic events of the coup and assassinations subsequently led to more back-to-back military coups in Nigeria.

The leaders of this first coup were the Ibo-speaking Major

With this few words I beg to support.

Senator (Mrs) B. U. Kerry : May I take this opportunity to thank the Federal Government who voted millions of pounds for the development of our country. May I also thank the Federal Ministers who worked day and night planning the development of this country. My special thanks go to our able and energetic Minister of Finance, Chief Festus Okotie-Eboh, who made this huge sum available. We women are particularly grateful for the thousands of pounds voted for women's organisations in this country. All these show that our Federal Government is always thinking of our women-folk.

I am now to appeal to our women to try all they can to co-operate with the Federal Government rather than to criticize them harshly. Kind, motherly and constructive suggestions will yield us better results.

The President : Are we all women ?

Senator (Mrs) Kerry : I am appealing to the women through you, Mr President, for we are part of the men's body. Senators know that a person has a whole body made up of many parts such as the eyes, feet, hands, and so on. As these parts are to a person so are women to men. Without the co-operation of the women with the men, the survival of this country will be difficult. Every Senator knows very well that where there is no woman there will be no nation.

On behalf of the women in this country, I register my deepest gratitude to the Federal Government for acting so kindly to all of us in this Federation. I pray that Almighty God will give us the great spirit of co-operation and tolerance which is the main-stay of our sex.

May I now appeal to the Federal Government to look into the behaviour of our girls who tend to lower the moral standard of this country by putting on very short and open dresses and going about almost naked. In my humble opinion as a mother, this is morally wrong and against our custom. It is not in our custom that we should go about naked.

Ghanaians have their own method of dressing. Indians have their own traditional method of dressing as well as the English. So do all countries of the world. One wonders,

therefore, who the Nigerian girls of to-day are imitating by putting on the short and unpleasant dresses I have referred to.

I am, therefore, appealing to the Federal Government to look into the way our girls behave nowadays. We, the parents of the nation are indeed ashamed of them. By checking all acts of immorality on the part of our girls we shall be building our nation in a correct and decent way. We Nigerians should popularise our traditional way of dressing by teaching our children how to wear our national dresses.

May I conclude my speech by emphasising the fact that our girls need more moral education because they will become mothers of the nation.

Thank you, Mr President.

The Minister of Mines and Power (Alhaji Yusuff Maitama Sule) : I rise to support the Second Reading of the Appropriation Bill. In doing so, may I, Mr President, on behalf of my Colleague the Minister of Lagos Affairs, be allowed to review, very briefly, the main aspect of the activities of the Ministry of Lagos Affairs and of the various Bodies whose general policies have been under the control of the Minister of Lagos Affairs during the past year.

I would, in the first place, say on behalf of the Minister of Lagos Affairs how happy I am to welcome Senators to the City of Lagos. The importance of Lagos in the economic, social and political development of the country was underlined by its being raised to the status of a City on 1st October, 1963. I am proud to have been able to say that what Senators wished for during the last Budget Session has become a reality even before this present Budget Session.

As Senators very well know, the Ministry of Lagos Affairs which works in close co-operation with the Lagos City Council and the Lagos Executive Development Board is responsible for providing Lagos with most of its vital needs and services. The development in Lagos and Nigeria over the last three years has been tremendous. This significant development has, quite naturally, created more than proportionate increase in the demand for essential services. The provision of these essential services for Lagos whose attraction to many people in the Regions is becoming

(32)

Senate speech by Senator Kerry, 1964

General Aguiyi Ironsi and the top Ibo army officers, Major Emanuel Ifeajuna and Chukwuma Kaduna Nzeogwu. General Ironsi then appointed his chosen Ibo generals to govern different regions and states of the country, thus giving the impression that the coup was a regional plot, by the Ibos, which it might as well have been. For instance, General Odumegwu-Ojukwu, an Ibo, was deployed to the Eastern region, later declared as Biafra. The ethnic origin of the top coup leaders also gave the impression that the Ibos were out to govern Nigeria on the basis of divide and rule. This resentment and misconception led to the start of the ethnic cleansing and the pogrom against the Ibos in Northern Nigeria. Millions were massacred.

My parents were still in Benin City when Eastern Nigeria seceded and declared the State of Biafra. This was in July 1967. The federal government of Nigeria did not want this to happen so war was declared on Biafra. This was eventually known as the Nigerian Civil War or "the Biafran War" and raged until 1970. Millions of indigenous Biafrans were killed in Northern Nigeria.

The bloodbath spread all over the country, carried out by those who harboured hatred or jealousies towards the Ibos for their industry, hard work and leadership qualities. So most Ibo youths fled home and joined the Biafran army. Those who did not join the army, stayed wherever they were in the country and fought back, however they knew best. The civil war was savage and the federal government was determined to crush Biafra and re-unite Nigeria.

During this war, various Western (European) governments supported whichever side they favoured but most were against secession. At a certain point during the war, Biafran forces invaded the newly created Mid-West State en route to Lagos and declared it the "Republic of Benin".

However the Republic collapsed a day later as Nigerian troops over-ran and overtook Benin City, chasing the Biafran soldiers back towards the east which was Biafra.

Mum, me and the grandchildren. Nicolette (right) and baby Nduka

The Biafran soldiers were now in retreat! As they fled east towards the River Niger, they sought refuge and support from sympathisers wherever they could find them. So it came about that when the Biafran soldiers arrived in Benin, they headed straight for St Paul's Ibo Church where my parents were based. My parents had no choice but to feed them, because although they imposed themselves on the church, my family's sympathy did lie with these young starving Biafran soldiers who were being pursued by the federal army. This contact with these brave fighters was to come back to haunt my parents as I will relate later.

An aspect of the Nigerian conflict could be attributed to language and different traditions. The Ibos on the West of River Niger (that's my people) spoke and still speak a dialect of the Ibo language, which probably explains my parents' sympathy with the Biafran soldiers, but my parents were mainly unhappy about the ethnic cleansing that was taking place in Northern Nigeria.

7: CIVIL WAR AND MILITARY TRIBUNAL

* * *

*"Whatever you do, or dream you can, begin it.
Boldness has genius and power and magic in
it."*
(Johann Wolfgang von Goethe, (1749-1832)

The war years and after were very tough for most of the Nigerian population including my parents. This time was especially difficult and painful for those who lost loved ones, jobs and all their material possessions. My parents had fled Benin City to their homeland, Owelle-Olubor, about forty miles east towards Asaba, following the advice of the kind Bishop Agori Iwe. He was a true friend to my parents and continued to appreciate their work. Whenever some women complained unfairly about my mother or her work, the Bishop rebuked them fairly and frankly, telling them they were "jealous of this woman", which of course was true.

The night after the Bishop advised my parents to leave Benin City, armed robbers invaded and attacked the vicarage. They arrived shooting into the air, shouting for my parents to open the door because they were soldiers. "Open, open, soldiers, open or you're dead!" They continued to fire into the air. Some were speaking in the Benin dialect, others were speaking pidgin English. My parents knew not to open the door! They prayed as everyone in the house began to pile furniture - tables, chairs, cupboards behind the front door and the back door in case these criminals attempted to break down the doors. To protect themselves further, my family dragged the beds from the bedrooms for the same purpose. Meanwhile, the whole household was screaming, and phoning the police and the Bishop simultaneously for help. Luckily, the armed criminals did not attempt to break down the doors or windows, which they could easily have done. As dawn broke, these criminals fled. No one knew why, but they simply fled as quickly as they came.

My parents left Benin City the following day with only the clothes they had on and a few precious belongings, such as family heirlooms and photo albums that they could quickly lay hands on. They lost everything and recovered very little, because their home at the vicarage was over-run and looted soon after, by, perhaps, federal soldiers and indigenous people. Many very valuable family heirlooms, photographs and documents were also lost. One of the most valued items was a beautiful black baby doll with sparkling brown eyes just like that of a real little girl. This doll was the size of an average-sized new baby and was given to my mother by Miss Ross when she had me. We loved and cherished the doll and called it "nwa baby" meaning "baby child". She always sat with the family photographs on our beautiful locally-made bookcase in the parlour. Visitors used to admire the doll, commenting on her smooth skin and beautiful dark hair. Having a doll like that was really quite unique at that time. It wasn't just my doll but every family member loved her. We all missed "nwa baby" very much and often wished the looters had taken something else rather than that precious doll.

1976, In London for Centenary celebration of the
Mothers Union. Mum – second from right (front)

As the Biafran war raged and escalated, many soldiers and
civilians were murdered or maimed. Millions perished and the
country was divided. People either sided with Nigeria or Biafra.
Everyone had or acquired a grudge and was seeking revenge but
Biafra desperately wanted its own state for its own people or
what was left of them. Most of the Ibo-speaking military
officers, including General Aguiyi Ironsi had been assassinated,
and those left were in hiding. Meanwhile the Nigerian soldiers
continued to drive back the Biafran soldiers.

Some African leaders and the new Nigerian military leaders,
including Lieutenant Colonel Yakubu Gowan (who was
supported in his campaign to become the head of state by
Northern military officers), were making efforts to end the war.
A summit of military leaders was held at Aburi in Ghana in
January 1967. This attempt to resolve the disagreement failed

and the war raged on until 15th January 1970, when Biafra surrendered and Nigeria declared victory.

Even as the war continued to be fiercely fought, and after the war ended, my mother's workmen were not far behind the soldiers, collecting spent ammunition shells, which were stripped of the brass around the casing and sold to feed the families. People tried to survive in any way that they could.

When the Nigerian federal government re-took Biafra and declared the war over, the administration decided to "bring to justice" civilians who they believed had supported "the enemy". "The Rebel Activity Tribunal", as it was called, was set up and one of those on the wanted list was my mother, for feeding Biafran soldiers during the war. Chief Justice Boyo, who was presiding over the tribunal, was the Bendel State Attorney General. The names of all the wanted people were denounced and announced repeatedly over the airwaves and they were urged to give themselves up. So my mother fled into hiding at her niece-in-law's home in the next village, Ute-Ogbeje, six miles away from Owerre- Olubor. She was with her niece-in-law, Adolie, for two weeks before she eventually gave herself up, following the advice of her lawyer and my father. She couldn't hide forever anyway and did nothing wrong. The tribunal lasted for six months. Barrister Stephen Giwa-Amu, later the Bendel State Attorney General, was my mother's Defence Attorney. The presiding Chief Justice at the trial, being aware of my mother's previous high office, integrity and innocence, released her to the jubilation of family and friends. My mother's ordeal may not be comparable to that of Joan of Arc who was burnt at the stake for her belief in 1431, but she had the same grit and felt the same sentiment that Joan felt when she (Joan) said that,

"Whatever I have said about my deeds and words in this trial, I let it stand and wish to reaffirm it ... I could not say anything different."

My mother couldn't have done anything differently either. Many people knew she was a pacifist and did not believe in wars. In giving aid to the Biafrian soldiers, she had been doing her Christian duty, and as the result of the tribunal confirmed, Mrs Kerry had no case to answer. She was trying to save lives.

My elder brother George and I were overseas while the Biafran war was raging. My brother was studying medicine and I was studying nursing, which I gave up to get married. My four children and I returned briefly to Nigeria in 1972. At this time, I could only manage the basic qualification from the UK Open University Foundation Course in English Literature, Art History and Music which I had studied in the UK shortly before our return. My parents were disappointed because they knew I had the academic ability to do whatever I wanted to with my life. So, my mother went into action! She encouraged me to go back to University. First, she paid my University fees for the first year at Ahmadu Bello University, Zaria and bought all my text-books for my University course. My admission was based on my Open University qualifications. My mother went to the Ministry of Education in Benin City to support my scholarship application, which I was awarded to complete my first degree in English Language and Literature in 1976. She also financed, totally, my Masters Psychology degree in 1978 in the UK, quickly followed by a Doctorate degree in Special Educational Needs in 1983 which was later completed on a Nigerian Federal government scholarship.

After the civil war in 1971, my parents were re-located to St John's Church, Agbor, a large town fifty miles east of Benin City. They had abandoned this post for Owerre-olubor at the start of the civil war. My father was now a Canon of the Anglican Church. My maternal grandmother, Rachael, was very elderly at this stage and though still strong, moved in with my parents. She died peacefully in my mother's arms in 1972, aged about 101 years. She blessed my parents to the end.

I would like to give some insight into my parents' work in Agbor. Their sojourn there brought many highs into their church ministry, as well as the worst lows. Hatred and malice reared their ugly heads.

Lagos 1965

The church grew with time. Both church and vicarage were modernised by my parents. The congregation of over a thousand appeared happy. Then suddenly, all hell broke loose, as a handful of the church members started seriously agitating against my parents. My parents "were overbearing," they lied, my parents "were not listening to [their] concerns and millions of Nairas were missing from the church coffer," which they didn't have in the first place, "drinks were stolen from the church" and so on and so forth. My parents couldn't understand what brought on this change of mood because they had treasurers who were in charge of finances as well as other checks and balances.

One of the agitators confronted my parents, telling them to leave Agbor as soon as they could because Jesus did so much good in the world and yet was crucified!

This nightmare came to a head when this bunch of dissidents (both men and women) plumped the depth of depravity by booing and heckling my father as he preached on Sundays. "Resign! Physician, heal thyself! Thief! Go away!" they would heckle! They went further by maliciously publishing on the front page of a national newspaper–The Daily Times– that my parents had embezzled millions of Nairas from the church. My parents were dismayed because the leader of this gang was a known public figure whom my parents thought was a friend. The church was divided; most people supported my parents and a few were on the other side. My parents stood fast anyway. The saving grace in all this was that the Bishop supported and believed in my parents, who in reality had done nothing wrong. The rebel ring leaders, about thirty of them, were excommunicated from the church. It was a great relief to my parents when these men and women eventually saw sense and apologised to the Bishop and the church. They begged to rejoin the church, and their plea was granted. My parents' stay became calmer and more fruitful. In 1977 my father was transferred to All Saints Church, Asaba (the capital of Delta State) as the first Archdeacon of Asaba Archdeaconry from where he retired in 1979. Asaba was a happy and peaceful posting for my parents. They loved the place and it was a worthy place to end their church ministry.

As my grandmother grew older, my mother made sure she was comfortable and wanted for nothing. My granny was always well-dressed, though unlike my mother, she wasn't particularly into fashion. She dressed in the normal Nigerian dress code:

usually a blouse and a big "rapa" round her chest or midriff. She was a local self-taught midwife and worked well into her old age. She could stop an impending miscarriage in its tracks with a dose of her home-made remedies. Through her knowledge of local herbs she delivered many healthy babies. She knew a lot about Nigerian herbs and medicines to treat all manner of illnesses: belly-ache, ear-ache, ulcers, heartburn, tooth ache and many more. My granny had put on weight in old age but still looked beautiful. She was plump and warm, serious looking but very loving. She was always telling us the story of her past. Whenever we were around her, my younger brother and I loved to snuggle beside her. She radiated love and pure spirituality, though she occasionally shouted at us for bad behaviour. She was alarmed and worried when my brother George informed her he was travelling to the UK for further studies. "Are you going to fly in that bird-like thing we occasionally see flying through the sky and who is going to look after you?" she asked.

My mother took great care of her mother, regularly sending her loads of food-stuff such as yams, rice, tins of palm oil, groundnut oil, bush meat and smoked fish as well as firewood and her favourite tobacco. My granny loved her clay pipe and would smoke in the evenings with her friends. Any food stuff she received would often be shared with her relatives and Christian friends. Her younger brother Nathaniel was a great farmer and also looked out for her. In fact they cared very much for each other.

In the 1960s, my mother pulled down her parents' mud house in Igbodo where she grew up and set up a pretty little bungalow built with bricks and corrugated iron sheets for her mother. My uncle Obed inherited the bungalow when my grandmother died and lived there until his death in 1983. Some of our relatives still live there. That environment still holds many memories for me, because of the link to my mother, my uncle and my grandmother whom we used to visit regularly as children.

8: VICTORY AND NEW BEGINNINGS

* * *

"Trust in the Lord with all thine heart; and lean not unto thine own understanding...in all thy ways acknowledge him, and he shall direct thy paths."
(Proverbs 3: 5-6)

My mother worked even harder as the years went by so her children could further their education overseas. To do this, she continued to travel in all weather, went hungry, slept in shacks in the bush, bought and sold produce and merchandise, made business contacts and continued skimping and scraping. My mother sometimes sent us fried chicken and roast peanuts (which she tinned herself) through friends visiting the UK.

There was great rejoicing when George returned from India as a qualified medical Doctor in 1972. Life was good again! My parents organised a huge welcome party for him, including a Church thanksgiving service. Many political heavy-weights at that time in Bendel State were invited and attended the service. They prayed for a blessed life and a good wife for George. The

Prime Minister, Dr Samuel Ogbemudia, chaired the occasion. My mother assisted her son with the purchase of his first car, a Mercedes Benz, as a congratulatory and welcome-home present. My brother began his medical career at the University of Benin Teaching Hospital, Benin City.

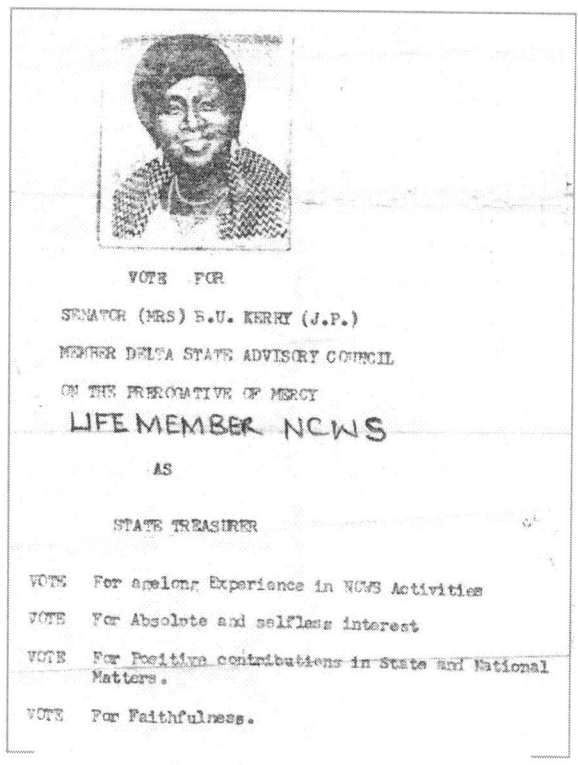

Campaign poster 1980

In 1976, the centenary celebration of the Anglican Mothers' Union world-wide took place in London. My mother was Bishop Agori Iwe's choice to represent the Benin Diocese at the centenary conference in the UK. That year was the hottest summer in the UK for a long time and my mother loved it. She stayed in Matlock, Derbyshire and was very well looked after by Mrs Saville of All Saints Church. My mother relished every minute of her visit. One of the highlights and something which made her very happy was going for tea with other visitors to Buckingham Palace and meeting the Queen! It was a remarkable occasion for her and a great achievement. Her business acumen never deserted her though, because she purchased a lot of Mothers' Union and other Christian memorabilia such as

With her Better Life programme secretary Mrs Kate Ufuegbuna (1980)

crosses, broaches, pens, writing pads, church books and booklets to sell and distribute to the churches in her Diocese of Benin City in Nigeria.

My elder brother was back once more in the UK at the same time, for a postgraduate course in medicine with his wife and first child. My mother, as usual, supported them financially as much as she could, and helped them purchase a car, to make their life easier. My mother was always there to help!

The privilege to represent the Benin Diocese in the UK was obviously a source of great delight to my mother. She always said with true joy that, "this opportunity for me was the will of God to glorify His name and serve him and I thank my Bishop for it."

There were women in the church who felt the Bishop should have picked them instead of Mrs Kerry. But the truth is that he had picked the hardest worker, the most reliable and most capable candidate, because the Bishop was himself a very capable and honest man. Often, when the church women and other clergymen's wives began to agitate against my mother, the Bishop saw through their spite and envy. The truth is that, people either, loved and admired Mrs Kerry or they did not; but mostly, people loved her.

From the late 1970s, my parents turned their attention to the development of my father's homeland Owelle-Olubor, and Igbodo, where my mother was born.

"We need a grammar school in Owelle-Olubor," my mother said one day to my father. "Good idea," my father replied, "I'm with you."

For a long time, their priority had been to bring a secondary school and a dispensary to rural Owelle-Olubor where my mother also spear-headed the building of a roofed market, to shelter people from the sun and rain. They could now pursue their dreams after my father's retirement in 1979. Owelle-Olubor Grammar School was built and opened in 1979. My mother in particular fought hard to bring this school to Owere-Olubor. She made regular trips to the Ministry of Education in Benin City, accompanied by at least four or five Owelle-Olubor chiefs and elders at a time, whom she often fed at roadside cafes. Quite often my mother would bring them to my house in Benin after their visit to the Ministry of Education. I would feed them happily, before they travelled back home to Owelle-Olubor. The head Chief,(old but tall and good-looking), known as "Ochibani" and other elders, including Nkwo-igwe, really relished and cherished those trips. They were proud of their strong leader. They would chant repeatedly in praise of my mother in our local dialect, "who is like Mrs Kerry?", "No one", "who do we trust?", "Mrs Kerry" "who will see us through?" "Mrs Kerry", "she is a woman stronger than a man!" They would all respond with cheers and clapping.

Next to be established in Owelle-Olubor was a Dispensary Health Clinic, a goal which did not take long to achieve, again, due to my mother's effort. Her warm and authoritative personality made it easy for people in the Ministry of Health to listen and to support her.

Owelle-Olubor never forgot my mother in life and in death. The appreciation shown at my mother's funeral on 11th June 2005 was phenomenal. The Owelle-Olubor Grammar School pupils and their teachers lined the funeral route from the church to the graveside (in our family compound) in memory and in honour of her work for the people, and in appreciation of her great efforts and achievements for the school. Two "Houses" or dormitories in the school were named after my parents, Archdeacon Kerry House and Senator Kerry House in remembrance of them. My mother was deeply mourned by the churches in Delta State and in the whole country, by those who knew her. Most of the clergy in Delta State, if not all attended my mother's funeral, forming a long procession to the graveside where she was laid to rest. Thousands more people filled the church, spilling out into the surrounding streets. Bishop Chukwuma of Enugu Diocese preached the sermon as requested by my mother. This honour was a source of great comfort to my family.

My mother set up her own maternity unit, ("Faith Maternity") as far back as 1969, on the ground floor of their home in Owelle-Olubor to support women with antenatal and postnatal care and also to mentor them in child and family care. My mother had great vision and always quoted Proverbs 29:18, "where there is no vision, the people perish." She was an initiator of great pioneering ideas. She was creative and practical. Two midwives were employed to manage the maternity and my brother, Dr George (who later moved to Lagos) visited from time to time to oversee the activities and nursing care. The maternity unit is now defunct, due to the proliferation of many 'health clinics' in the area.

The loss of my beloved father to a stroke, aged 77, on 21st July 1981 was a huge set- back for the family. My mother found it extremely hard because my father was her rock, her right-hand man, and her greatest admirer. My father was very ill in the end and my mother nursed him with great love and dedication to the end. My mother slept every night on a small bed she had set up in the room beside my father and would get up before 6 am every day to give him a bed-bath, change his clothes and feed him. She would comb his hair and make him comfortable, either sitting up or lying down. He would smile his gentle smile and say "dalu" (thank you). My mother lost her best friend and though she held her emotions together, she mourned her loss till the end. In between caring for my father, she never forgot caring for others. Towards the end of his life, my father was very sad, not because he knew his life was coming to an end, but because my mother was going to be left on her own. One night, lying on the next bed beside my father as she had done since his illness, my mother heard whispering voices as if my father was having a conversation with someone. My mother was taken aback. She did not stir but concentrated hard to hear what was being said. My father kept repeating, "But what about my wife? She is alone." After further whispering for about three minutes my father said, "all right. If it is your wish - - - " and fell back to sleep. I was in the house that night and my mum rushed into my room to tell me what she heard. She never asked him who he was talking to because she knew how sad and worried my father was to be leaving her behind!

My father often said that my mother was a wonderful role model of what a wife and a mother should be. He loved Proverbs 31: verses 10-29, a Bible passage he always said epitomised, and to me, still epitomises my mother's life:

"Who can find a wife of noble character? For her value is far more than rubies.

The heart of her husband has confidence in her and he has no lack of gain.

She brings him good and not evil all the days of her life.

She obtains wood and flax and she is pleased to work with her hands.

She is like the merchant ships; she brings her food from afar.

She also gets up while it is still night and provides food for her household and a portion to her female servants. She considers a field and buys it from her own income, She plants a vineyard. She begins her work vigorously and she strengthens her arms.

She knows that her merchandise is good and her lamp does not go out in the night.

Her hands take hold of the distaff and her hands grasp the spindle.

She extends her hand to the poor and reaches out her hand to the needy.

She is not afraid of the snow for her household, for all her household are clothed with scarlet. She makes for herself coverlets; her clothing is fine linen and purple.

Her husband is well-known in the city gate when he sits with the elders of the land.

She makes linen garments and sells them, and supplies the merchants with sashes.

She is clothed with strength and honour and she can laugh at the time to come.

She opens her mouth with wisdom and loving instruction is on her tongue.

She watches over the ways of her household and does not eat the bread of idleness.

Her children rise up and call her blessed and her husband praises her:

Many daughters have done valiantly but you surpass them all!"

My father's funeral was remarkable too. It was attended by the Prime Minister of the State, Professor Ambrose Ali and his wife, along with various top politicians and church leaders. My father's life was also extraordinary, because he achieved so much in his own right and had shone a great light into some of the darkest places in the world. His life was full of sacrifices and genuine dedication to the work of God. He loved people, especially children but can also discipline them when necessary. My parents often dreamed of opening a Kindergarten (Nursery) and a Primary school in Owerre-Olubor. This dream is currently coming into reality with the Gift of Grace Education Project Charity for disadvantaged 5-12 year olds in Owerre-Olubor which I founded in 2012. My brother Patrick had built (in 2003) Archdeacon Kerry's Chapel, (in memory of my father), at Mary and Martha Girls' Secondary School in Igbodo, Delta state.

Mother's Union Centenary 1976

In December 1985, my mother was appointed a member of the Board of Governors of Owerre-Olubor Grammar School, a job she cherished and worked hard for till the end. This was followed in 1986 by an appointment as a member of the Assessment Appeal Tribunal, for Ika Local Government. She was made a Justice of the Peace (JP) in the same year.

Aged seventy-six, my mother was still very strong and active and committed to the causes she was passionate about. She was at the forefront of the Better Life Programme for Rural Dwellers ("Better Life" for short) Workshop on Women in Rural Development in Nigeria. This programme was launched in Abuja, Nigeria in September 1988, designed at that time by the Babangida administration to revolutionise the lives of rural dwellers. My mother was at that launch.

The Better Life Programme for Rural Dwellers encouraged rural women in various Local Government Areas to launch diverse projects to support themselves and the government efforts to help them. These projects encompassed food farming, garri processing, yam /plantain /cassava flour processing, rice milling, fruit processing, fish farming, cloth weaving and developing ceramic and small-scale industries and brick moulding. In short, the aims and objectives of the programme were:

"1. To encourage rural women to improve their environment and standard of living

2. To achieve a more fulfilling life for rural dwellers and their families.

3. To focus more on self-development in education and income-generating activities"

However, the jury is still out on whether this programme made any difference to rural life in Nigeria! In fact, Heinrich Stiftung, in his article, 'Nigeria; Women on The Sidelines' (2008, p.3), states that:

London Mother's Union Centenary 1976. Mum is standing first right

"all the gender machinery put in place by the government to integrate women into the development process had a record of being faulty. The Better Life Programme's aim was to create new empowered rural women, but ended up reinforcing gender subordination in the guise of women's activism, like The National Council for Women Societies (NCWS)."

However, Mrs Kerry embraced the "Better Life Programme" wholeheartedly and with her team of local women, founded the Otu-Odinonyemma Farmers' and Weavers' Society Limited in her Ika Local Government Area. This was an association of rural women determined to set up a project to grow and manufacture rural products, like aluminium utensils, producing palm kernel, palm oil and palm kernel oil for soap-making. This organisation was issued with a certificate of incorporation in May 1988. In the same year, my mother was appointed a member of the "Mass Mobilization for Social Justice, Self Reliance and Economic Recovery" programme for the state ("MAMSER" for short). MAMSER, like Better Life, had grand goals, to build:

"1. a united, strong and self-reliant nation

2. a great and dynamic economy

3. a just and egalitarian society

4. a land of bright and full opportunities for all citizens

5. a free, democratic society."

Wole Ademolekun (1992) General Manager, Corporate Service Petroleum Products Pricing Regulatory Agency, Abuja, Nigeria.

My mother was simultaneously co-ordinating the Bendel East Zone Better Life Programme, mobilising women, arranging payments of Better Life subsidies, organising sales of products, and farming and making aluminium cooking utensils herself. As well as being an accomplished businesswoman, my mother was an excellent farmer too.

Rural women were awarded small grants in order to facilitate these ventures. My mother mobilised and encouraged Ika women to plant, sow, harvest, weave cloth, produce and market palm oil and palm kernel and make pots and pans from aluminium. Any small-scale enterprise was encouraged and supported by my mother.

As the women's leader and founder of the Otu-Odinonyemma farmers and weavers Society, my mother encouraged her group to purchase a kernel-cracking machine from their grant money so they could harvest and sell palm nuts for export. While oil for cooking was extracted from the fleshy cover of the palm nuts, the nuts would be cracked to separate the hard outer shells from the inner nuts, usually exported for the oil which is extracted for manufacturing products like soaps and body lotions.

My father left fifty-eight hectares of palm kernel plantation in his will for the family. This land, a mile from the family home, was acquired by my father with the approval of his people in 1948. They were very proud of him, he was proud of his people. Over the years, my parents covered the plot with palm kernel trees and this has always been referred to as "ani nkwu papa" (papa's palm plantation).

The idea of a nut-cracking machine was intended to ease and quicken the women's efforts of sitting all day cracking nuts by hand with a small stone on a larger stone. First of all, the women needed an outhouse to store the machine to be purchased, but there was a dilemma because they had nowhere to set up an outhouse. So my mother offered them a small plot behind the family home where an outhouse was eventually built for the machine the women dreamed of. The oil processing and palm kernel cracking machine was eventually purchased at the cost of 61,978 Nigerian Naira (about £300) from the Project Development Institute (PRODA) in Enugu, Eastern Nigeria under the directorship of Mr Kaine. However, PRODA did not come to install the machine for a long time. After a period of two years and twenty-eight visits involving thousands of Nairas, the machine was eventually installed. It took many more trips to Enugu for Mr Kaine and his men to visit Owerre-Olubor to activate the machine. Meanwhile, the interest on the bank loan for the purchase of the machine continued to rise. Rather than activating the machine at Owerre-Olubor Mr Kaine and his men removed the machine to Enugu. For many months all attempts to retrieve the machine failed. A women's delegation sent to Enugu to investigate what had happened to their machine, found it being used to produce vast quantity of palm oil for PRODA customers at the Institute premises. Helpless in the face of this atrocity by PRODA, my mother and her secretary, Mrs Kate Ufuegbune wrote letters of appeal to the Federal and State Ministers of Science and Technology for assistance but no one was listening. As a last resort, PRODA was taken to court by Mrs Kerry and her Otu-odinionyenma Women Farmers' and Weavers' Co-operative Society Ltd.

After a protracted court case and more lawyers' fees, PRODA was found guilty of theft and ordered to pay the Co-operative Society, one million Naira, (about £4,000). This was never paid. My mother and the society members were on their own. No one spoke up for them, but this was one nut my mother couldn't crack! So, the women's dream of benefitting from the Better Life programme in order to gain financial independence died. The machine was never returned and remains in Enugu!

Life carried on regardless. Age did not deter or dim my mother's energy for achievements and in 1989 she won first prize in the Better Life Exhibition in Lagos. Most of these exhibits were comprised of locally-made products, such as, aluminium pots and pans, hand-woven cloths and farm produce, like yams, rice, beans and vegetables. She was awarded a shield and a Certificate of Merit, which contributed to Bendel State winning second prize overall in the exhibition. My mother was also made an adviser to Bendel State government on Better Life for Women Affairs, to assist the Bendel State government in their work in this area. The following year, 1990, she was awarded the Nigerian Association of Women Journalism (NAWOJ) Star Award Certificate in recognition of her Inspirational Contribution to the Development of Bendel State Womanhood.

Mrs Kerry was truly "a woman for all seasons". With her dignified, elegant and sparkling demeanour, she could fit in with the great and the good, as easily as she could get on with local women in the local market. Still, she was a dominant and respected figure wherever she went.

OTUODINONYEMMA BETTER LIFE FOR
RURAL DWELLERS,
MULTI PURPOSE CO-OPORATIVE
SOCIETY,
OWERRE/OLUBOR/UMUNUDE,
IKA LOCAL GOVT. AREA,
BENDEL STATE.

14th December, 1990

The Hon. Minister of Science and
Technology,
Federal Republic of Nigeria,
9, Kofo Abayomi,
Victoria Island,
Lagos.

Dear Sir,

A LETTER OF APPEAL

We are a group of helpless women representing the above named
society. We are appealing to you through our President Senator
Mrs. B. U. Kerry J.P. to save us from the deliberate frustration of
our co-operative society by Mr. Kaine the Project Director, Project
Development Institute (PRODA), Enugu. Apart from the fact that this
institute is under your Ministry, every one in this our great country
knows that PRODA is your baby. You nutured it from its childhood to
the present international rating.

We paid PRODA under Mr. Kaine's Directorship the sum of N61,975
(Sixty-one thousand, nine hundred and seventy-five naira) for an oil
processing and palm kernel cracker machines including charges for
installation and maintenance. After a period of two years during which
we paid more than 28 visits involving thousands of naira on transport to
Enugu, the machines were eventually installed.

It took us many more trips of appeal to Mr. Kaine at Enugu to send
his people to come and make the machines operational. Unfortunately the
then Military Governor Col. John Mark Inienger could not commission the
mill, due to this delay on the part of PRODA. In the meantime the interest
on the Bank loan for the purchase of the machines continued to increase.

Rather than sending his people to come and make the machines function, Mr. Kaine sent his workers to come and take the machines back to
Enugu under the pretex that certain faults in the machines are to be
corrected, and promising to bring back the machine in another months time.
(See Mr. Kaine letter attached).

To our greatest surprise Sir, we now went back to Enugu one month
after the date promised for the return of the machines, only to find our
machine being used to produce warious quantities of palm oil for customers
at the institute's premises. Sir, at the sight this disgraceful "rip off"
I broke down in tears, because I have never experienced this type of
fraud and sabotage in all my services to this nation.

Asked why he treated us with this kind of disregard, the Director
Mr. Kaine said they wanted to offset their personal expences incured while
building the machines, which they could not have achieved by being
truthful to us, and that we can go to hell, he does not care.

Honourable Minister Sir, we prefer crying to you rather than going
to hell. We feel that your intervention in this matter is necessary,
otherwise we stand a good chance of not seeing our machine again. Your
personal intervention will show our soceity the seriousness of the
Federal Government about the success of the Better Life Programme, as
well as instill sanity into people like Mr. Kaine, who has betrayed the
trust reposed in him, and his coleagues by the Federal Military Government,

Letter of appeal

Persecution and victimisation of women, in various forms,
continued apace in Nigeria. These forms of oppression included
women being falsely accused of witchcraft or of responsibility
for their husband's death, or being held responsible rightly or

wrongly for their inability to bear children. Often a wife suffered and still suffers the pain and humiliation of her husband sleeping with a house-maid or takes a second wife in order to bear a longed-for son. In fact it is fairly common in Nigeria for husbands to ill-use and oppress their wives because they could get away with it, whatever religion they practised. The list is endless. My mother was having none of it and worked endlessly for justice for brutalised women.

In 1989, my mother saved a woman called Obi from Igbodo from being lynched as "a witch." This poor frail skinny victim, wailing her innocence, was carted off, against her will by some chiefs and elders of her own village to a remote village called Ishiagwu, many hours away from her home, to be tried for witchcraft. Ishiagwu had one of the "agaba" shrines where people accused of witchcraft were taken to be found out or set free by "juju" high priests. "Juju" is a fetish, amulet or any inanimate object, attributed with supernatural powers. Obi was accused of repeatedly killing her enemies' babies, even though these babies often succumbed to all manner of tropical infections and diseases such as malaria, diarrhoea and malnutrition. It is noteworthy that those usually accused of witchcraft were women, often poor, and alone. Obi's daughter, Ada, came to my mother, sobbing and wailing, to report what had happened to her mother. This was the sort of fight my mother relished! She was incensed! She summoned her driver to take her to the village where Obi had been taken. Usually, on arrival, amid loud drumming and chanting, these victims were quickly given a very strong concoction of alcohol-infused tobacco and Indian hemp roots to sedate, confuse or intoxicate them and render them helpless. This brew, typically sent victims into a trance and hallucinatory state, inducing false confession of the crimes they did not commit. They were then shamed and booed out of town!

By the time my mother arrived in "Ishiagwu village" (where Obi was taken), Obi was very agitated and thrashing about on the ground, "confessing her sins," in front of the high priest's thatched hut, encircled by jeering animated villagers. More of the libation she was given was set aside in a large clay jug to be administered until she confessed all. The high priests and villagers were all in a frenzy, drumming, singing and screaming, "get up, dance, confess, confess, witch, witch!" to the sound of drums. The dazed woman was surrounded by these hounds when my mother arrived. As soon as she got out of her car, she could hear the chiefs saying, "Mrs Kerry is here, Mama Kerry is here," and many of the villagers quickly dispersed because they knew or had heard of my mother. By now, Obi was totally confused, and couldn't recognise my mother whom she knew well.

After the chiefs and so-called high priest had offered the usual polite greetings, as was customary, such as, "mma nne; Mama yabia?" (respect, mother; you've come?), my mother, in her usual authoritative manner, asked in our dialect "what is going on here?" The high priest, face caked in white native chalk, eyes wild and demented with chanting, was fanning himself with a goat-skin fan. He replied with a sense of achievement, "Mama, we've got a witch here!"

"What witch?" my mother asked, visibly angry.

"This woman is a witch and has attacked many babies at night", the priest continued, "She is still confessing and will totally confess when she has taken another cup of our palm wine."

At that point my mother ordered the larger-than-life head high priest to drink half the potion himself, so Obi could finish the rest as they had stipulated. When the high priest refused, my mother threatened them with the police. The whole process came to an abrupt end!

They were ordered by my mother to let the woman go. Obi was helped into my mother's car and they drove home. The Ishiagwu villagers, who had gathered to be entertained, couldn't believe what they had experienced and the Igbodo people couldn't believe their eyes when Obi returned home. If my mother hadn't intervened and Obi had been found guilty by the mob, which was a certainty in this case, her life would have been a living hell because it would have been impossible for her to live with that stigmatisation for the rest of her life. Many lives have been ruined this way! If someone is not popular in the village, does not mean she is a witch. This practice of falsely accusing poor, sometimes, sick and lonely women of witchcraft, had long been abolished in rural areas of Delta State but was still practised for money by some desperate villagers and fetish or "juju" priests.

My mother was always at the forefront of battles like the one I have just narrated in support of women and wives, who had been ill-treated, subjugated and humiliated by their husbands and society at large. On a number of occasions, she actually physically sent packing, troublesome house-maids and girl-friends. My mother would insist they left the marital home immediately. Husbands often agreed with her, because in most cases, these guilty husbands did mend their ways afterwards, apologising for their misdemeanours to their wives and children. My mother was a fearless fighter for truth and justice and wrong-doers were afraid to confront her.

In the context of a Nigerian marriage, men are rarely seen as guilty even when they err, because women generally are brought up to believe in their own inferiority, and usually marginalised and oppressed. "As we raise our heads", states Susan Griffin (2000, p.40) writing generally about women "we are reminded of home, sameness and tradition. The history of mankind is a history of repeated injuries and usurpations on the part of man towards woman." My mother knew and saw that the Nigerian husband does not know it all and that the opposite was true. She realised early in her life that women are the heartbeat of the universe. Every human being is born of a woman. Women are built to bear children, to nurture, to love, to teach and to guide and if given the opportunity, do it excellently. In addition to this, my mother encouraged wives to love and respect their husbands.

My mother's compassion stretched beyond support for suffering women. Her deceased nephew's son, Benji visited my mother in tears in 2002, because he was supposed to be returning to college but had no money for his fare let alone the tuition fees. My mother was very moved because she had great love for her late brother and his children and grandchildren. She sent Jerry her Ghanaian live in care-taker to call Mallam (an Hausa trader and family friend). She did business with Mallam, selling and buying coral beads. The corals she had purchased from him previously, she begged him to buy back. This money she gave to Benji, to enable him return to college. It covered both his fare and college fees. Benji now lives in Europe, a happily married family man who regularly tells the story of my mother's love and kindness in his time of need.

More honours were bestowed on my mother as time went by. In 1990 she was appointed the Bendel East Matron of the Voluntary Work Camps Association of Nigeria, and also was made the third member of the board of Trustees for Sickle Cell Anaemia in the whole Bendel State.

As the years rolled by, my mother's accomplishments were more and more recognised and further awards and honours rolled in. From 1991 until 1992 my mother was a member of the Delta State Commission for Women's Affairs and was made treasurer of the National Council for Women's Societies until 1994. She was the only lady member of the Delta State Advisory Council for the Prerogative of Mercy. This is a law council set up by the state government to provide for the establishment, composition and factions of an advisory council on the Prerogative of Mercy and for purposes connected with it, such as pardoning of murderers or for the amendment of the local Government Laws and other Bills of Delta State. Thus, my mother's life work and recognition continued to grow.

In 1996, I brought my mother to the UK for rest and medical care. She did so much for me that I can never repay her love for me and my children. During her time in the UK, she made a great impression on the nurses and doctors who cared for her at the BUPA private hospital in Cardiff. The medical staff regularly commented on her complexion, youthfulness and charisma. Her orthopaedic surgeon, Mr Pemberton, who gave her a new knee, sometimes brought his lovely little daughter, on his rounds and he was very kind and warm towards my mother. Before leaving the room after his regular visits, the surgeon would ask little Sarah to "kiss Mrs Kerry goodbye". Sarah was a lovely girl and easily and always obliged. I thought it was a wonderful way to bring up a child in a multi-ethnic society! Mr Hawkesworth, the eye Consultant, Dr Wiltshire, our GP (General Practitioner) and Mr Ellis, our optician were equally kind and caring towards my mother.

One of the `BUPA staff nurses, Barbara Morgan was also very kind and friendly and exceptional in the care of my mother. After my mother left hospital, Barbara asked my mum and me whether she could use Mrs Kerry for her case study "A Patient's Research" (1997). We agreed and she got to know my mother even better

Below are some extracts from Barbara's work:

"Mrs B [for 'Bernice' as my mother was referred to in hospital] arrived in Britain in July of this year (1996) to receive treatment in order to alleviate pain in her arthritic joint. I assume she came here to receive the expert ministrations of a specialised surgeon. Documenting her (Mrs Kerry's) life has been a privilege for me, and has given me an insight into

Nigerian life of which I knew little. Her mind is still sharp and her memory acute and her pleasure at being able to recount some of her past gave me great pleasure too. There are many of her achievements not listed here in my work, suffice it to say that her personality speaks volumes of the person that she is".

She continued, "I nursed Mrs B and through body language and English we built up a rapport. She had a youthful face for her age, dark brown eyes that shone and a broad smile that showed enviable white teeth. Mrs B was a delight to nurse, we could greet each other with a warm hug and so our friendship began. Permission was sought to document Mrs B's life history and this was granted by mother and daughter."

The nurse concluded, "The value of this to me was that I had no possible idea of the achievements, happiness and trauma, that had been Mrs B's life until our in-depth conversation. I feel that as nurses we should be an advocate for the elderly patient, many of whom may well have enjoyed lives that may have been significantly more fulfilling, rewarding or even traumatic than our own. Therefore respect and dignity must be maintained at all costs."

I was really very gratified to read what a total stranger thought of my mother. My mother never forgot Nurse Barbara even after she returned to Nigeria and Barbara never forgot my mother. They kept in touch through me and I'm still in touch with Barbara.

My mother continued to age "elegantly" and "beautifully", as my brother Patrick used to say. People looked up to my mother even more as she advanced in age, seeking her advice on various issues, asking for funds and asking her to endorse this or that document for them. She was happiest when helping people and when surrounded by them. People often sat round her to learn more. Her charisma, childlike glow and conspicuous beauty shone like a beacon to the end. She blazed a trail for women in politics and in society as a whole. She stood for the truth at all times. She was a formidable political activist, an independent spirit and an incredible pioneer for women in politics. She was feared, loved and respected in equal measure. The many deserved accolades and trophies she received in her time and after her passing are a tribute to her hard work and achievements. She received a posthumous award in 2006 for all her life's achievements. This was a Delta State award for "Distinguished Women in Politics".

As far back as the mid-1960s, there was a plan in the Anglican Church to split Benin Diocese into three Dioceses: Asaba, Ika and Benin. From 1966 until 1977 when these dioceses were created, my mother was the only female member on the committee for this process. After the division of Benin Diocese, my father was transferred to All Saints Church, Asaba in 1977 as the first Archdeacon of Asaba Archdeaconry. This deserved achievement of becoming an Archdeacon was what my father had worked for all his professional life and he was very thankful to God that he got there in the end. My observation of the Anglican Church in Nigeria today is that every Tom, Dick and Harry (or Okonkwo, Okolie and Okafor!) who enters the Church wants to be an Archdeacon or Bishop immediately but does not understand the full implication and meaning of such a privilege. They want big houses and cars. The saddest aspect of it is that many have no love of the church or their congregation and only care about what they can gain for themselves.

By virtue of my mother's status as Secretary of the old Benin /Anglican Diocesan Women's Conference (1962-78), she was a representative at all the meetings of the Diocesan Board of Benin during this period.

In February 1979, my mother was appointed a Customary Court Judge in Bendel State, after a stint as a customary Court member (1970-74) and a councillor (1975-78) for The Ika Local Government area. She received many congratulatory letters from many eminent people including, Mrs Akinluyi, the

Archdeacon's wife at that time, for the above achievement. True to form, my mother was a popular but formidable Customary Court Judge, with clear vision. Florence Shinn, in "The Game of Life and How to Play It" (1925, p.24), stated that, "clear vision is like a man with a compass; he knows where he is going" and "if you believe in yourself, others will believe in you". My mother was a sound believer in herself!

In one land dispute, in 1979, my mother, as a judge, gave a minority landmark judgement in the Customary Court which was upheld on appeal at appellate Courts by the High Court of Justice in Agbor and was reflected by Justice Oki when he published a Nigerian law book in 1980.

Many husbands in the rural areas often neglected their wives and gave them scant attention. These wives were often given very little or no money for food, nor were they given enough crop seeds from their husbands' own piece of land to grow and harvest. Instead, these husbands would give their wives only tiny portions of land to farm, with no seeds or crops to sow and yet expected lavish meals to be served to them day after day, never mind feeding the children. If meat was killed or bought, the men had the lion's share. Eggs were beyond the reach of what children could expect to enjoy. Such inequalities, my mother stated categorically, were wrong. My mother believed children's welfare must always come first in families and wives should be given adequate support to nurture the family.

As already stated in previous pages, my parents continued to finance George's education in the UK, as well as my own education overseas. They also took care of Patrick's education in Nigeria. When I returned temporarily from the UK in 1972 without a degree, my parents were disappointed but encouraged me to go back to university and financed my education up to Doctorate level. They cared for and nurtured my children in my absence. My mother was always making sacrifices for her children and grandchildren, both physically and financially, and was always very encouraging.   Through her consistent encouragement and support my brother Patrick qualified as a lawyer and graduated from Lagos Law School in the late 1980s.

9: CHAMPION OF WOMEN AND THE VULNERABLE

✳ ✳ ✳

"... It is more blessed to give than to receive..."
Acts 20:35

From the narrative so far, it is clear that Mrs Kerry was a religious, social and political activist. She was an advocate for the weak, the vulnerable, the defenceless and the oppressed and did not count the cost to herself.

Recognition for my mother's work stretched as far back as 1963 when she won a Leadership Certificate, for her leadership work in the church. Over time she rightly deserved all the accolades, trophies and honours that came her way. She cared about people and was a nurturer. She never raised her hand to her children or anybody else's children for that matter, though she participated in the upbringing of many children as well as her own. She used to say," but what part of a tiny body can you hit, without doing some damage?"

I think of my mother as the wind that blew us high to fly. If someone upset any of us, she would say with encouragement, "and what is that to you? Just get on with your life". My parent's guiding principle, which they passed on to us, was their belief in truth, honesty and hard work and they practised these values throughout their own lives.

My mother was definitely our first teacher. She taught us from an early age to read and write and sing. She would sit with my younger brother and I, listening to us read, correcting our mistakes and teaching us the right spellings. She taught us from an early age our dates of birth, to spell and write our names and told us their meanings too. For instance, George spelt: G-e-o-r-g-e, Grace: G-r-a-c-e and Patrick: P-a-t-r-i-c-k. She practised sports with my brothers when they were little (I didn't like sports, still don't), especially running and the high jump. For high jump she would drive two sticks, four feet apart into the soil, with an extra one across them. She would jump the first rung as an example for my brothers' to copy, then continue to raise the bar as they progressed higher until they could jump no further. I believe this early activity built my brothers' interest in all kinds of sports. My mother was very competitive in sports at school, a quality my brothers inherited.

The first hymn my mother taught us as children was "Oh God, our help in ages past". It still brings a lump to my throat when I hear it. This hymn was in a small New Testament Bible, given to each of us as children by a visiting white missionary, Rev Barnard. My mother's philosophy until the end was that, " education is the way". She was always ambitious for herself and her children, with a passion for beautiful things and beautiful people. She always said she was very lucky to be surrounded by her beautiful family and people used to say to her, "what a beautiful family you have." Her great desire was for people to be happy, and she lavished praise where praise was due. My mother constantly showered me with love and praise, calling me the sweetest of names in her rich warm beautiful voice: Ada (first daughter), Egi (coined from Grace), Titi (baby girl) and

Nnem (my mother). It is common in my culture for parents to call their children "papa", "daddy", "mummy" or "nnem" (mother) and so on, as a sign of great affection. How I miss all that! Her life was wholly directed towards the love and support of others. She was full of knowledge, both learned and self-taught.

As an educator and philanthropist, my mother helped many families to educate their children. She either paid the fees when parents could not afford them or led the parents to the relevant contacts where they would get the appropriate help. On one occasion, when taking a boy called Christopher to college for an admission interview in 1979, they were involved in a serious car crash, which they survived. My mother supported and paid school fees for the education of many of her nephews and nieces, both on her side and on my father's side of the family, at various points during their education. One of the letters written to my mother by one of these nephews, still remain. In this letter Paul laments my mum's minor accident at that time, wondering, as my mother continued to recover, who would be paying his school if anything adverse befell my mum. Not all of the people she helped showed any appreciation but it mattered very little to my mother. She was happy to help at people's darkest hour of need. Her greatest strength was that she cared very much about people.

She was a beacon of light for everyone around her. She was always giving generously to the sick, the needy, the church and the community at large. St Barnabas Church, Owerre-Olubor benefitted the most. She clothed the poor, fed the sick and comforted the weak. My mother once bought material (for our traditional attire) at Christmas for all of the women and their children in "ogige ndi-uka," the church compound in her childhood home, Igbodo. It was not just the church women (who knew when and how my mother was born following the arrival of the missionaries) who loved her, the entire village loved to see her because of her charm and constant generosity in handing gifts of food, clothes and money to them. The older generation in the village particularly cared about her because they always remembered her as a child. During the first Christmas after my father's death, though in deep mourning, my mother slaughtered two huge sheep which were distributed around my father's neighbourhood as a gift to all.

My mother comforted many sick or dying people who specifically asked to see her. So did those in other difficult situations. Her reassuring presence and prayers were so soothing, people always testified. She had acute presence of mind, and was quick-thinking. Once at their post in Agbor, my father tripped and fell in the front garden, dislocating his elbow. My mother was immediately with him, shouting "don't move, don't move!" She helped him up and pulled the elbow back into place before taking him to the doctor's. She had a sharp instinct of what to do in an emergency, especially when anyone around her was taken ill. A relative of ours, Uje, suffered from severe depression (not known in our culture as such) for months in the 70s. She sought and found refuge with my parents who cared for her for over three months at their Parsonage in Agbor. Uje suffered from severe anxiety and was very frightened of almost everything. She lived with them free of charge, just eating and resting. This lady often testified to the care she received from my parents, especially my mother, who also paid secondary school fees for two of Uje's children.

Moreover, how many mothers could afford to send a nanny all the way from Nigeria to London (in the 70s) to help her daughter, who had just had a new baby? My mother made that sacrifice for me.

My mother was godmother to many children and adults. She understood the meaning and responsibility involved and these parents believed in her. If there was any tough decision to make or any important person in government to see, people came to my mother and she very rarely failed in her mission. She would not be dissuaded by phone calls when a request she had made was refused or by soldiers at the gate of government Ministries. People in authority had great respect for Mrs Kerry and rarely could say "no" to her. Age never dimmed her razor-sharp intellect, and people continued to seek her opinion and advice into her nineties. She loved life and was generous to the end. Even at that stage of her life, she would offer gifts and money (for food or fares for travel) to those who came to visit her if she thought they needed help. If she had visitors during meals, she would willingly share her meals with them. She was youthful and sophisticated to the end, never losing that infectious hallmark child-like giggle and her beautiful smile.

My mother passed away peacefully on 15th April 2005, aged nearly ninety-three years. She had sixteen grand children and two great grand children. The likes of my mother are not often born into this world. They come perhaps once every century and what a privilege that she was my mother and born into the Nigerian community! The many tributes paid to her before and after her death illustrated the amazing life she led.

Her loss was akin to a huge light and warmth going out of our lives. My mother had an extraordinary and an unbelievable life! She had a pure and formidable aura about her. My father used to say that my mother was so remarkable that her enemies dissolved into smiles when they came face to face with her even if they had planned to kill her.

The family home in Owerre-Olubor was planned and built by my mother, with constant support and encouragement from my father. She was the power behind the throne! Her integrity and authority were always evident.

My mum and I, 1982

My mother's knowledge of many things was staggering! For instance, if someone wanted to build a house, they would ask her advice. She would ask how many bedrooms they had in mind and would proceed to tell them exactly how many bricks or blocks would be needed to build the house. She was also a very tidy person. My father used to call her bedroom "UAC" (United Africa Company), after the store where African cloths and household materials were sold in colonial days. She arranged all her "rapas" and "jorges" (materials for sewing traditional outfits) and blouses meticulously. There was a place for everything: coral beads, gold and other kinds of jewellery neatly packed in their containers and shoes and sandals in their places. Frocks and blouses hung on hangers. She was always so organised that no matter how late she got home at night or how tired she was, she always put things away tidily.

Like my maternal grandmother, daily prayers were very important to my mother. She was very religious and spiritual, always praying before meals, before going out, and at night before bed.

"Better Life" rally 1980

Her favourite hymn was "What a Friend We Have in Jesus". I cannot exhaust my mother's many attributes which included her radically independent mind and spirit. She was courageous, tireless, determined, highly principled and stood for truth and justice. She was recognised as an outstanding personality, embodying all that is good in a human being. Mrs Kerry's positive qualities were many. It is no exaggeration to say that my mother was, driven, generous, funny, honest, dynamic, energetic, charismatic, articulate, loving, cheerful, fair, forgiving, and encouraging. Her laughter was beautiful, embracing people in its warmth.

My mother's death was, and still is, the most traumatic experience of my life. I remember thinking "who will love me now and who will pray for us?" Though an indomitable spirit had been silenced, her legacy lives on. By writing my mother's biography, I hope to make a contribution to filling the gaps in the history of the role that Nigerian women played in politics, and to redress the imbalance and inequality of how women have often been left out, erased or ignored when histories have been written.

MY MOTHER used to say:
Never forget your smile.
Avoid bitterness
Believe in yourself
Never assume you know everything

Me, my brothers and Bishops 2003

10: MORE ACCOLADES

* * *

*"The humility and fear of the LORD are riches
and honour." Proverbs 22:4*

A number of chieftaincy titles were conferred on my mother during her senatorial years, although she never used them. For example, she was made Chief of Okpila and Dauda (Elder) of Fuga in 1965, and the Ada of Ndobu village, in Igbodo, in her later years, as a mark of honour from her people. The title of "Ada" was akin to being made a Baroness or a Dame in the UK. As well as being a Justice of the Peace (JP) she was conferred the honour of the Knight of the Order of St Mary in 2003. Her other awards are as follows:

1988: First prize in the Better Life Exhibition in Lagos, and was awarded a Shield and a Certificate of Merit.

2001: A shield awarded for Political Activism by the Ministry of Women's Affair.

2002: A shield awarded by Delta State Government for Political Activism

2002: An award for political excellence by the Delta State Government for her long-standing political activism.

2003: A similar award by the Delta State Ministry of Women's Affairs for her contribution to women's welfare in the state.

2005: A posthumous Delta State Award for Distinguished Women in Politics.

2005: The Governor of Delta State, Governor Ibori, commended my mother's distinctive service in his letter of condolence at her passing.

2005: The Federal House of Senate also mourned her passing.

2005: The Ukuokpolokpolo, the Oba of Benin, sent delegates with his special message of condolence.

2005: As the Ada of Ndobu, Igbodo (her birth place), the community mourned her passing in a letter of tribute.

Many past Nigerian women politicians hardly get a mention in written social and political histories of the country, but Mrs Bernice Kerry, Mrs Wurola Esan, Mrs Margaret Ekpo and other activists were cited by Dr J Shola Omotola in his article, "What is the gender talk about after all?, Power and politics in Contemporary Nigeria" (2007, p. 37).

"Women are mothers", he wrote, "producers, home managers, community organisers, social, cultural and political activists." He concluded that a few female politicians have had a mention here and there "but that's about it". Heinrich Stiftung in his article, "Women on The Sideline"s (2008, pg. 2) also states that "women's political participation in the early political life of the nation (Nigeria) was very minimal. Public marginalization seemed the order of the day. In the early years of independence, politics in Nigeria was more or less a man's affair. Only an insignificant number of women played prominent political roles in parliament. In this period, there were only four female legislators: Mrs Wurola Esan and Mrs Bernice Kerry in the Federal Parliament while Mrs Margaret Ekpo and Mrs Janet Mokelu were in the Eastern Nigeria House of Assembly. In northern Nigeria, it was only in 1976 that women received franchise to participate in voting." These citations gave me hope, that at least a few people have noticed the discrepancies which might one day be rectified.

The marginalization of women in Nigerian politics has continued apace but apart from my mother being a beacon of light in many aspects, she was a positive force for religious, social and political change in Nigeria.

So why are there still very few women in Nigerian contemporary political life and why are the few that ever participated rarely ever mentioned or remembered? Why are African women in general and Nigerian women in particular, so marginalized in politics? Again, Dr Omotola in his article (2007, p. 37) cites the two first women senators in Nigeria's first Republic – Mrs Bernice Kerry and Mrs Wurola Esan. Not many Nigerians have ever heard of or know these names, even though these women contributed so much to political debates in the House of Senate as cited in the Hansard of the period. Women have always been seen and portrayed as the weaker sex, often marginalised, oppressed, alienated, not taken seriously and sometimes despised. They were perceived only as child-bearers, but people forget the old adage that "the hand that rocks the cradle rules the world". This is true whether the woman or the mother in question is educated or not. The woman is the heartbeat of the world! Every human being is born of a woman!

Mum with Dr Ifeanyi Okowa, present governor of Delta State, 2003

As stated in Chapter 8, Nigerian political leaders came up with the idea of the "Better Life Programme for Rural Dwellers" in 1987, aimed at family development, improving healthcare delivery for families, developing family life and women's overall well-being. Did it work? It was helpful up to a point, because at least rural women in particular were very engaged with it initially, believing it brought hope and sustenance. However, in reality, this project was riddled with drawbacks. The programme was politicised, which led to rural women being more marginalised, with corruption and nepotism still rampant in politics. An example of one of these draw backs, was what the PRODA management in Enugu did with the Otu-Odinonyemnma Farmers' Union kernel-cracking machine. Even to date, as confirmed by Dr Omotola (2007, p.41) "women are still at the fringes of Nigerian political life and yet not many speak up for them".

I am convinced that the best way forward for women in Nigeria is a sound education, so that they could learn more about their role in society as well as in the home. Men should also be encouraged to support their wives. My mother never went to university but she was more knowledgeable than many who have gained a Ph.D. She was determined to make an impact, grabbing every positive opportunity that came her way and maximising such chances for the benefit of others. She empowered herself to do so much, and empowered others to help themselves.

There were many more women of my mother's era, such as Mrs Agatha Ehiemua (1920-2005) of Ishan town in Bendel State who actively contributed to Bendel State and the subsequent carving out of Edo State. Mrs Ehiemua made a significant impact on Nigerian religious, social and political life. She founded the "Ishan Women's Progressive Union" and became its first president. She was a businesswoman, and together with my mother, she was contracted to plant grass on some road kerbs in Bendel State. Mrs Ehiemua was nominated as a councillor to serve the Okpegho Local Government in Bendel State in 1976, and was honoured by the Pope with a medal in 1975. She was also a building contractor who played a leading role in acquiring some land from the Oba of Benin to build the State Secretariat Complex in Benin City. Mrs Ehiemua was a philanthropist and cared very much for the welfare of others. She single-handedly educated her two sons to university-level and was a Justice of the Peace (JP) and a member of many important organisations in Edo State of Nigeria.

Similarly, Mrs Fumilayo Ransome-Kuti (1900-1978), the musician Fela Kuti's mother, was another remarkable activist in her own right. She led her fellow Egba women in Western Nigeria on a campaign against arbitrary taxation. Mrs Ransome Kuti fought for suffrage and equal rights for all Nigerian women. She was prominent in the anti-colonial movement and was an activist, an educationist and a trained teacher. She was the treasurer and later president of the Western Nigeria National Council of Nigeria and the Cameroons (NCNC) a political party founded by Dr Nnamdi Azikiwe, who later became the first President of the first Republic of Nigeria.. She was an outstanding leader of Egba women in Western Nigeria and held a seat in the Western House of Chiefs of Nigeria as an Oloye (traditional chieftaincy title) of the Yoruba people. Mrs Ransome Kuti founded the Federation of Nigerian Women Societies. She gave women a voice.

Mrs Ransome Kuti died in 1978 from injury she received from an unjustified attack by some government soldiers

There are many more wives and mothers in Nigeria who supported their husbands in bringing up their children or worked single-handedly to help their children reach the highest professional levels. There are many unsung female pioneers throughout Nigeria, who through big business enterprises or small-scale trading, or farming, weaving and other odd jobs, contributed to raising doctors, lawyers, engineers and other highly qualified professionals.

SENATOR Bernice Unuango Kerry, 89, Nigeria first female politician to rise to that position and Chief Felix Ozere Osubor (JP), 91, pioneer Minister of Agriculture and Natural Resources in old Midwest Region are among the few surviving political activists who fought for Nigeria's independence and held exalted political positions in their hey days.

Sunday POINTER reporter, BENSON OKOBI during the week spoke with the esteemed senior citizens in their country homes at Owerre-Olubor and Umunede respectively in Ika North East local government area of Delta State.

Excerpts

Senator (Mrs.) Kerry

Sunday POINTER Madam, how will you compare politics in your own 'time with politics of today'?

Answer: Politics of old is not like politics of today. In our own time we were not after how to enrich ourselves, but we were after the affairs of the public - how we could control them, rule them and make them feel alright and lead them through the right path. We were after all these things. But the reverse is now the case for the present day politicians through the right path. We were after all these things. But the reverse is now the case for the present day politicians.

Question: Are you saying that all politicians are only after how to enrich themselves?

Answer: In fairness not all, but most of them are interested in enriching themselves to the detriment of those they are supposed to be representing and the reverse is now the case for the present day politicians. You know in olden days when we go about to campaign for votes we don't give money; the voters themselves don't demand for money. But nowadays politicians buy votes by giving money to voters to vote them into power. Some of them do this. When they happen to win and start officialising in whatever capacity the next thing in their minds is how to get back the money they spent in buying votes and other expenses they might have incurred during their campaign periods. Immediately they go in they want their money, like our own time we don't give money, but when they see you are a good person they vote for

> " Politics of old is not like politics of today. In our own time we were not after how to enrich ourselves, but we were after the affairs of the public - how we could control them, rule them and make them feel alright and lead them through the right path. We were after all these things. But the reverse is now the case for the present day politicians"

you to represent them.

Question: As an old politician do some of these new breed politicians come to you for advice?

Answer: No, they never come, because when they come I will tell them the real thing to do. So they don't come to me in that way (meaning advice). But when they come they only just chat with me as an old politician. But they don't come that you may give them advice not to give money or not to do that because without it they can not function properly.

Question: Have you been abreast with current happenings in the country? What I mean, following what

have been happening in the country?

Answer: As an old woman I am

Question: How old are you, ma? When were you born?

Answer: I will be 90 by June 12 next year. I was born in June 12, 1912. But despite my age I still follow the goings on in some aspects of politics.

Question: Like what?

Answer: (Pause for a while and smiled) Women that is my area of emphasis. They are very few in politics and the few women participating are being marginalised by their male colleagues. Our women in politics - some of them are not vibrant enough

Some are trying though. They should give them chance.

Question: Wasn't not like that in your own time?

Answer: (Shakes her head) No, no,

Question: How many were you in the house of Senate? I mean women Senators and how...

Answer: (Cuts me short). Oh, we were just only two - myself and late Wuroba Esan, the fire-spitting and fearless politician. We challenged the men when we sat them deviating. I wonder if our female politicians can do that now.

Question: But don't you think it is because of their few number?

Answer: (Laughs) How many women were in politics in our own time. We were few but simply wonderful.

Question: You wanted to say something before that question. What were you trying to say?

Answer: Yes, is about widows, old people and the youths. They are not well taken care of by the government. The various levels of government should make adequate provision for them us done in England.

Question: How do you assess Governor Ibori's and President Obasanjo's administrations in the last two years?

Answer: From all I have heard Governor Ibori has done. I think he is trying. The same view I have for Mr. President. Like I said the widows, old people and the youths should be well taken care of. Obasanjo is trying.

Question: Tell me a little about yourself and your family?

Answer: My husband is late Venerable Archdeacon G.I. Kerry, Archdeacon of Ika and Asaba respectively. Late Mrs Flora Azikiwe formerly Miss Flora Ogogbunam was my classmate at St. Monica's Secondary School. Ogbunike, I have two sons and a daughter. The first is Dr. G.I. Kerry, a medical practitioner based in Lagos; another one is Barrister P.O. Kerry, a director in Niger Delta Development Commission representing Delta State in Port-Harcourt and Dr. (Mrs.) Grace E. Okoh (nee Kerry) based in Cardiff, Wales. The beauty queen of Nigeria for the year 2000, Miss Mathida Kerry, is my grand daughter, one of my grand daughters.

Thank you Madam,

Thank you too, my boy.

Continued on Page 11

11: EPILOGUE: WOMEN OF NIGERIA

* * *

"There are two ways to spread happiness;
either be the light who shines it or be the
mirror who reflects it."
Edith Wharton (1862–1937)

My mother's remarkable journey spanned nearly ninety-three years and she spread great joy and happiness. Her profound wisdom and great insight, as well as faultless intuition and judgement helped many. She was always self-assured, with an enchanting presence.

Though my mother achieved so much, she would never have done it so magnificently without the love and support of my father. My father was always beside her and always very proud of his wife. There was no jealousy and no competition! Many Nigerian women were not, and are still not, so lucky in their marriages. This is because of issues that they face such as poverty, total dependence on their husbands and child-rearing practices. So, women's achievements, both within and outside the family, exist in relation to their men.

The image of the Nigerian woman is that she has a strong independent mind, yet she exists in the midst of a society riddled with poverty and unemployment. Often, Nigerian society uses the woman's strength both overtly and in subtle ways to discriminate against her. Though the Nigerian woman often found and still finds herself in situations that constantly challenge and undermine her self-sufficiency, she draws on her own strength to confront and overcome those obstacles that threaten her well-being.

Mrs Kerry and two of her grandchildren in the back garden

A good example of such a scenario is the "Better Life Programme" of the 1980s. The project was conceived by economic planners, without any input from the rural dwellers who were to implement the programme and benefit from it. It was focussed on the provision of infrastructure and physical resources and was not linked to national economic goals and priorities. As such, the "Better Life Programme" had no positive lasting effect on the lives of the women who were supposed to be its beneficiaries. This is not a total condemnation of the Programme, because it did boost the morale of the rural dwellers at that time, especially the women. However, women are still generally exploited as cheap unskilled labour and for the most part, continue to struggle on their own to support their husbands and children.

In spite of these tensions and frustrations in their lives, women still persist in their efforts to live the best lives they can, working hard for their children and their families. This determination rewarded women like my mother well. Such women reached the top of their professions and attained powerful positions, during a period when few women had the benefit of any kind of education or recognition. Many women in Nigeria today are still aspiring to achieve professional success and other fulfilments in all fields and in various capacities. These women are all champions and role models.

It is important that both the formal and informal contributions of women to the Nigerian economic sector should be acknowledged, encouraged and supported. Work has always been an integral part of women's lives and self-esteem. It has given them access to money and a sense of independence in a society where they couldn't always depend on their men-folk for financial support. Moreover, it has given women power within marriage, which is very significant because marriage is a vital aspect of Nigerian culture. Likewise, work has given women authority within their families, and on a wider scale, it has given them a higher status within their communities.

Confirming this, Knowles and Mercer (1992, pg111) state that:

"Nigerian women did not challenge marriage or the family as legitimate forms of social organisation. They did not see the family as oppressive to women and it was not considered acceptable to live outside family cultures. Their concerns were mainly land reforms and rural development."

So, women could be wage earners in the private or public sector, or small-scale farmers or petty traders hawking their wares in the streets with their babies strapped to their backs.

Urban and rural women alike are all involved in various forms of economic and income-earning activities but these are not included in the official labour statistics. There is an obvious need for consistent statistics of the contribution of these hardworking but "invisible" women. The Nigerian government still needs to work towards involving women in the reduction of poverty and unemployment in order to improve the quality of life of the population at large and to eradicate persistent poverty and redress the problem of social and gender inequality.

Mrs Kerry worked hard to ensure Nigerian women were given recognition and benefits commensurate with their important role and contributions to society. Many men, as well as women, in Nigeria still find it difficult to imagine women in a non-traditional role. The woman is still perceived solely as a housewife and child-bearer. So it is vital that we continue to champion access to better quality education for women. This was my mother's aim and belief. She firmly believed that "in educating a girl, you not only transform her life, but that of a whole community". She was a living example of that. Even more so, education helps a woman to learn more and earn more which reduces the risk of her children dying in infancy. It is a well-known fact that 28% of girls in sub-Saharan Africa are not in primary education and in Nigeria today, over 4.5 million girls are not in school ("The Teacher" magazine, March/April 2011, p. 21). In August 2011, the Nigerian Minister of Women's Affair and social Development, Hajiya Zainab Maina stated the obvious, by declaring that over 4 million school-age girls in Nigeria are not in school. In her nation-wide campaign, Hajia Maina maintained that "rapid progress in girl's enrolment, retention and completion will have to double if Nigeria is to meet the Millennium Development Goals of achieving gender parity in education and improve their (girls) participation in socio-economic and political development of the nation".

My mother prayed and hoped that these poor statistics in girls' education would improve with time. She was both the light that spread truth and happiness, and the mirror that reflected it, and her influence can still be felt in Nigerian social, religious and political life today, especially in Delta state.

A POEM FOR MY MOTHER

MY MOTHER

She is my first, great love.
She was a wonderful, rare woman - you do not know; as strong, and steadfast, and generous as the sun.
She could be as swift as a white whiplash, and as kind and gentle as warm rain, and as steadfast as the irreducible earth beneath us.

D.H. Lawrence, 1885-1930 (Inspiring Quotes about Mothers, 2000, p.14)

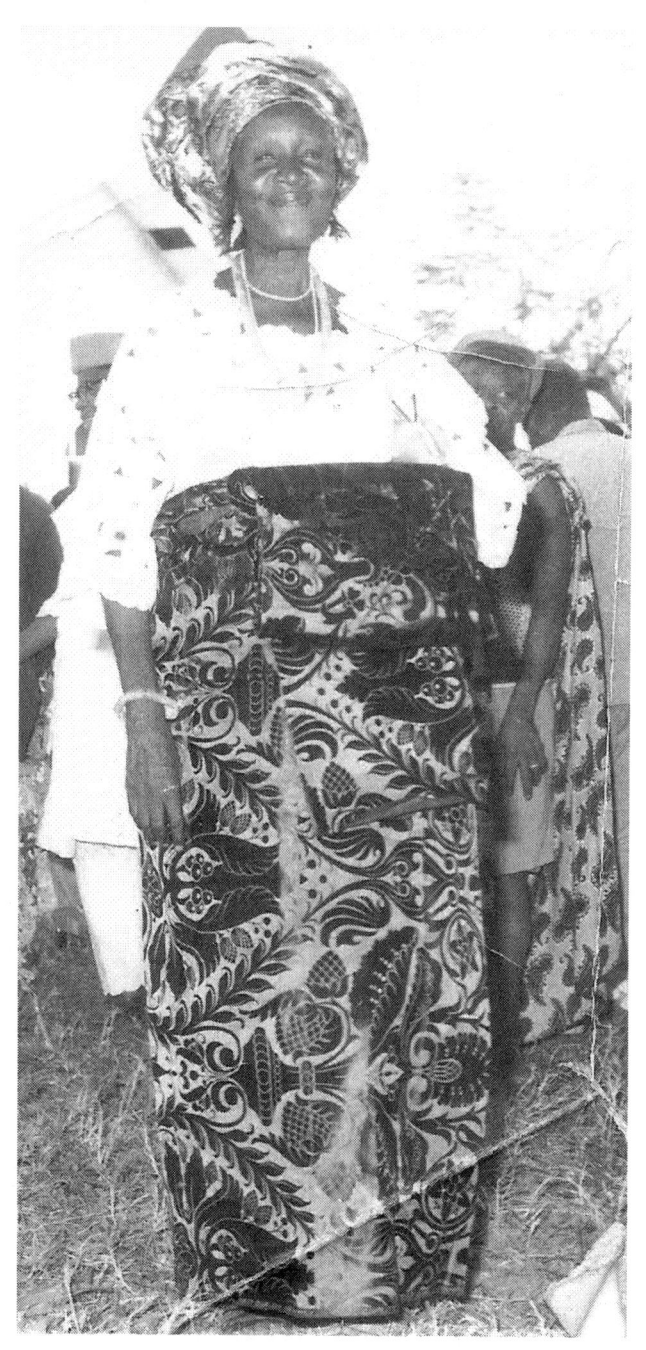

Mrs Kerry aged 75

BIBLIOGRAPHY

Achebe C, (1958) Things Fall Apart, London, Heinemann Publishers.

Ademolekun Wole with Tayo Ekundayo (2007), Interactive Public Relations, Ibadan, Spectrum Books.

Archdeacon Kerry's Family Archive.

Azikiwe Nnamdi (1971), My Odyssey: An Autobiography, New York: Praeger.

Burkland Paul (1939) Oh my papa: A lyric, Switzerland

Deutsch Helene, (1944): The Psychology of Women, Vols. 1&2 New York: Grune and Stralton.

Dowden Richard, (2008) Africa: Altered States, Ordinary Miracles, London, Portobello Books.

Equino, Olaudah (1789): The Interesting Narrative of the Life of Olaudah Equiano, USA, Dodo Press

Falola Toyin, Ed. (2005), Nigerian History, Politics and Affairs: The collected Essays of Adiele Afigbo, New Jersey, Africa World Press Inc.

Federal Republic of Nigeria Parliamentary Debates, Senate Official Report, (Volume13, No.9, Tuesday 14th April 1964): The Ministry of Information, Printing Division.

Glass Bob, (2003) Be Not Afraid – How to Conquer Your Fears, UK, Synergy Publishers.

Griffin Susan, (2000) "Woman and Nature": The Roaring Inside Her, San Franscisco, USA, Published by Sierra Club Books.

Ibuje Joan, (1982) Famous Women, Associated Press, Nigeria.

Knowles Caroline and Mercer Shamila, (1992)Feminism and Antiracism in 'Race', Culture and Difference, Edited by James Donald and Ali Rattansi, Sage Publication in Association with the Open University.

Malloch Douglas, (1925) Someone to Care: New York, Wise Parslow Co.

Morgan Barbara, (1997) a Module: Care of the Elderly, BUPA Private Hospital, Cardiff, United Kingdom

Murray T. Douglas (1902) as quoted in Jeanne d'Arc, maid of Orleans, Deliverer of France, Published by William Heinemann, London.

Nigeria Mamser Handbook, (1987) Nigeria, Published by the Directorate for Social Mobilisation.

Nigerian Federal Govt, (1987) Better Life: Bendel Rural Women at Self-Help Projects, Nigeria, Published by the directorate of Women Affairs.

Omotola Shola, (2007) 'What is this Gender Talk about after all?' in Gender, Power and Politics in Contemporary Nigeria, African Study Monographs, vol. 28(1) 33-46, April 2007.

Orizu Nwafor, (1993) The Leadership We want, Nigeria, Horizontal Publishers.

Scovel-Shinn Florence, (1925) The Game of Life and How to Play it: USA, Published by Simon and Schuster.

Shakespeare W. (1623) Hamlet: UK, Published by Nicholas Ling, First Folio.

Stifstung Henrich Boell, (2008) Article - Nigerian Women on the Sideline.

The Bible – King James Version, (Quotes)

The Teacher Magazine, (March/April 2011) article, 'Send my Sister to School', Published by The national Union of Teachers (NUT) UK.

To My Mother with Love, (2003) UK, Published by Marks and Spencer.

Wikipedia 2016: the free Encyclopedia

Printed in Great Britain
by Amazon

29842435R00097